The British Novel, Defoe to Austen

A Critical History

Twayne's Critical History of the Novel

Herbert Sussman, Series Editor
Northeastern University

The
British Novel,
Defoe to Austen
A Critical History

John Allen Stevenson

University of Colorado

Twayne Publishers
A Division of G. K. Hall & Co. • *Boston*

PR
851
.S687
1990
157863
Feb. 1993

The British Novel, Defoe to Austen: A Critical History
John Allen Stevenson

Copyright 1990 by G. K. Hall & Co.
All rights reserved.
Published by Twayne Publishers
A division of G. K. Hall & Co.
70 Lincoln Street
Boston, Massachusetts 02111

Copyediting supervised by Barbara Sutton.
Book production by Gabrielle B. McDonald.
Typeset in 10 pt. Palatino
by Huron Valley Graphics, Inc., Ann Arbor, Michigan.

First published 1990.
10 9 8 7 6 5 4 3 2 1

Library of Congress Cataloging-in-Publication Data

Stevenson, John Allen.
    The British novel, Defoe to Austen : a critical history / John
Allen Stevenson.
        p.   cm.—(Twayne's critical history of the novel)
    Includes bibliographical references.
    ISBN 0-8057-7852-7
    1. English fiction—18th century—History and criticism.
I. Title.   II. Series.
PR851.S687   1990
823'.509—dc20   90-4374
                                                                    CIP

To my parents

Contents

Preface

This study is meant to convey something of my enthusiasm for the eighteenth-century English novel. My hope is that such enthusiasm will prove useful and pleasurable for both the beginning student of the period and the specialist. It has become increasingly difficult to write for both these audiences, and I have made choices that may, at times, displease one group or the other. I have deliberately limited the number of novels I discuss because I prefer to develop what I think are important ideas in some detail. This approach has meant I could not treat such undeniably significant writers as Tobias Smollett, Fanny Burney, and Ann Radcliffe. With equal deliberation, I have kept scholarly arguing to a minimum, and I have generally tried to use the notes either to suggest some of the places where a curious student might go to seek further development of an idea, or to acknowledge my particular debt to someone else's work. Occasionally, too, I have indicated where I disagree with a prominent point of view.

But books not only are made up of other books; they also emerge from a community of other people. It is a pleasure to acknowledge those who have helped make this one possible—though of course they have no responsibility for any of its flaws. Some of the material in chapter 2 originally appeared in an earlier form in the Winter 1981 issue of *ELH* as "The Courtship of the Family: Clarissa and the Harlowes Once More"; it reappears here with the kind permission of the editors. A version of chapter 5 was delivered as a talk to the English Department at Duke University in March 1989; my thanks to that distinguished group, and especially Regina Schwartz, for their warm hospitality and stimulating response.

This study had its distant beginning as a dissertation on Samuel Richardson, written at the University of Virginia under the direction of Ralph Cohen and Leo Damrosch. I owe both of them a considerable intellectual and professional debt—as I do the late Irvin Ehrenpreis. At Colorado, I am grateful to a number of people, for a variety of help: Alan Andersen, Les Brill, Marshall Brown, Steve Epstein, Jim Kincaid, Paul Levitt, Anita Menking, Jeffrey

Robinson, David Simpson, Bob Steiner, and Keith Thomas. Marje
Urban processed and reprocessed my words with speed, accuracy,
and good cheer. The wonderful students who took my classes in
the early English novel in the fall of 1987 heard early versions of
these ideas and kept me honest and motivated. The general editor
of this series, Herb Sussman, has been remarkably generous with
his time and experience, and this book is better for his help.
Throughout, my wife, Jillian, was my steadiest encouragement and
faith, and my happiest inspiration. My gratitude to her, and to my
parents, will always remain my deepest pleasure to acknowledge.

John Allen Stevenson

University of Colorado

Chronology

1731 Defoe dies.

1737 Theatrical Licensing Act.

1740 Richardson, *Pamela* (vols. 1 and 2). James Boswell born.

1741 Fielding, *Shamela*. Richardson, *Pamela* (vols. 3 and 4).

1742 Fall of Walpole. Fielding, *Joseph Andrews*.

1743 Fielding, *Miscellanies* (including *Jonathan Wild*).

1744 Pope dies.

1745 Second Jacobite rebellion. Swift dies.

1747 Richardson, *Clarissa* (vols. 1 and 2).

1748 Richardson, *Clarissa* (April, vols. 3 and 4; December vols. 5–7). Smollett, *Roderick Random*. John Cleland, *Memoirs of a Woman of Pleasure (Fanny Hill)*.

1749 Fielding, *Tom Jones*.

1750 Johnson begins *The Rambler* (through 1752).

1751 Fielding, *Amelia*. Smollett, *Peregrine Pickle*.

1752 Fanny Burney born. Charlotte Lennox, *The Female Quixote*.

1753 Smollett, *Ferdinand Count Fathom*. Richardson, *Sir Charles Grandison* (vols. 1–4).

1754 Fielding dies. Richardson, *Sir Charles Grandison* (vols. 5–7).

1755 Johnson, *Dictionary*.

1756 William Godwin born.

1757 Edmund Burke, *A Philosophical Inquiry into the Origins of Our Ideas of the Sublime and Beautiful*.

1759 Johnson, *Rasselas*.

1760 George III accedes to throne. Sterne, *Tristram Shandy* (vols. 1 and 2).

1761 Richardson dies. Sterne, *Tristram Shandy* (January, vols. 3 and 4; December, vols. 5 and 6).

1762 Smollett, *Sir Lancelot Greaves*.

1763 Boswell meets Johnson.

1764 Ann Radcliffe born. Jean-Jacques Rousseau, *Emile*. Walpole, *The Castle of Otranto*.

1765 Sir William Blackstone, *Commentaries on the Laws of England*.

Sterne, *Tristram Shandy* (vols. 6 and 7). Bishop Thomas Percy, *Reliques of Ancient English Poetry.*

1766 Oliver Goldsmith, *The Vicar of Wakefield.*

1767 Sterne, *Tristram Shandy* (vol. 9). Maria Edgeworth born.

1768 Sterne, *A Sentimental Journey.* Sterne dies.

1771 Smollett, *Humphry Clinker.* Henry Mackenzie, *The Man of Feeling.* Smollett dies. Sir Walter Scott born.

1774 Lord Chesterfield, *Letters to His Son.*

1775 American Revolution begins. Jane Austen born. Matthew Gregory Lewis born.

1778 Burney, *Evelina.*

1781 Johnson, *Lives of the Poets.*

1782 Burney, *Cecilia.*

1784 Johnson dies.

1789 French Revolution begins.

1791 Boswell, *Life of Johnson.*

1794 Radcliffe, *The Mysteries of Udolpho.*

1795 William Godwin, *Caleb Williams.*

1796 Lewis, *The Monk.* Burney, *Camilla.*

1797 Radcliffe, *The Italian.*

1800 Maria Edgeworth, *Castle Rackrent.*

1804 Napoleon crowned emperor of France.

1811 Austen, *Sense and Sensibility.*

1813 Austen, *Pride and Prejudice.*

1814 Austen, *Mansfield Perk.*

1815 Battle of Waterloo. Austen, *Emma.*

1817 Austen dies.

1818 Austen, *Northanger Abbey, Persuasion.*

Introduction

Consider the following passages:

I shot at a great Bird which I saw sitting upon a Tree on the Side of a great Wood, I believe it was the first Gun that had been fir'd there since the Creation of the World; I had no sooner fir'd, but from all Parts of the Wood there arose an innumerable Number of Fowls of many Sorts, making a confus'd Screaming, and crying every one according to his usual Note; but not one of them of any Kind that I knew.

O Lovelace! if you could but be sorry for yourself, I would be sorry too— but when all my doors are fast, and nothing but the keyhole open, and the key of late put into that, to be where you are, in a manner without opening any of them—O wretched, wretched Clarissa Harlowe!

Hushed be every ruder Breath. May the Heathen Ruler of the Winds confine in iron Chains the boisterous Limbs of noisy *Boreas*, and the sharp-pointed Nose of bitter-biting *Eurus*. Do thou, sweet *Zephyrus*, rising from thy fragrant Bed, mount the western Sky, and lead on those delicious Gales, the Charms of which call forth the lovely *Flora* from her Chamber, perfumed with pearly Dews, when on the first of *June*, her Birthday, the blooming Maid, in loose Attire, gently trips it over the verdant Mead.

—I was shewing Mrs. *Bridget* our fortifications, and in going too near the edge of the fossé, I unfortunately slip'd in.—Very well *Trim*! my father would cry,—(smiling mysteriously, and giving a nod, but without interrupting him)—and being link'd fast, an' please your honour, arm in arm with Mrs. *Bridget*, I dragg'd her after me.

And then the figure, turning slowly round, discovered to Frederic the fleshless jaws and empty sockets of a skeleton, wrapt in a hermit's cowl. Angels of grace, protect me! cried Frederic recoiling.

—Don't I hear another carriage?—Who can this be?—very likely the worthy Coles.—Upon my word, this is charming to be standing about among such friends! And such a noble fire!—I am quite roasted. No coffee, I thank you, for me—never take coffee.[1]

1

One central problem for all critics of the eighteenth-century English novel (and for the purposes of this volume, Jane Austen will be included in that group) is clearly illustrated by these quotations. It is an astonishingly diverse form, and its early, great practitioners seem to know implicitly a truth that D. H. Lawrence, writing much later in the genre's history, spelled out this way: "You can put anything you like in a novel."[2] You can put in Defoe's remarkable combination of the tangible and the vague, gifted as he is with the ability to make us feel we are there without in any way interfering with our own imaginative contribution. Or Richardson's ventrilo-quism, which allows us to overhear a young girl's post-rape delir-ium. Or Fielding's mock-heroic apostrophe, or Sterne's lewd innu-endo, or Walpole's ghost, or Austen's Miss Bates, rattling on her endless quotidian reportage. All these voices—and many more besides—are part of that wide universe of possibility that opened to these and other writers when England fell in love—not, it should be said, without apology and hesitation—with those long works of prose fiction that we call the novel.

My emphasis in this study will not be on where the novel came from. That much-fretted question has inspired some of the eighteenth-century novel's best critics, but it has also limited them. The assumption has been that such an origin, rightly understood, can provide us with a definition of the form that, in the words of one of the most recent and resourceful of these critics, will "compre-hend" (meaning both understand and include) Richardson and Fielding.[3] These two novelists are singled out for reconciliation not only because they were bitter personal rivals but also because the obvious differences in their fictional art have made a comprehensive definition of the form seem especially problematic. The urge to bring them (and the rest of their cohorts) together is a worthy one, attempt-ing as it does to show that beneath artistic difference and personal animosity there is some deeper unity. Contributing to this urge, too, is the complaint, old as the novels themselves, that no reader or critic can do justice to both Richardson and Fielding, that the very sensitivities that open up the beauties of one man blind a reader to the merits of the other, and vice versa.[4] But that may be a truism to cherish, rather than a problem to solve. Therefore, I will not seek an origin or a definition that "comprehends" all early English novels; instead, I will pursue and, where possible, celebrate the diversity that the passages just quoted begin to suggest.

What I intend to do in the chapters that follow is to try to sketch that diversity by focusing primarily on one aspect of the novels I will survey: heroism in *Robinson Crusoe*, power in *Clarissa*, language in *Tom Jones*, laughter in *Tristram Shandy*, politics in *The Castle of Otranto*, and courtship in *Emma*. These novels are so rich that it would be impossible to attempt anything like a complete reading of any of them in so small a compass. But I hope the sum of all these particular emphases will be more than simple arithmetic would allow. For example, Crusoe's heroism becomes an occasion for exploring the heroic possibilities of the genre in general, while the examination of the psychology of power in *Clarissa* opens a perspective on the pleasures of character analysis. In other words, I have tried to explore questions that resonate with issues in the period and in the novel form as a whole. What I hope to achieve is an overall picture that can suggest something of the variety of these fictions but will also provide a sense that, however wide and flexible, there are frameworks of possibility within which they exist. For instance, Samuel Johnson, in his *Dictionary*, defined the word *novel* as "a small tale, generally of love."[5] The procrustian tendency of those who struggle to define what a novel is has rarely been so clearly revealed. What I will try to do instead is discuss ways in which novels (which are about many things besides love) tend to share a certain family resemblance when they do take love for their subject. That ambition is, of course, a smaller one than attempting a comprehensive definition of the form, but I hope it is also more honest about the actual experience of reading novels. One recent commentator on the criticism of the eighteenth-century novel has shrewdly remarked, "I wonder if . . . cheerful acceptance of chaos is not only the easiest but the wisest course."[6] But "chaos" implies a value judgment I hesitate to accept—let's call it "diversity" and be glad.

The present moment is an especially exciting time to reexamine these novels. A recent book was entitled *The New Eighteenth Century*,[7] and there is a feeling abroad in the critical world that the modes of reading provided by literary theory make the eighteenth-century novel look very different from the way it did, and thus open it up for rethinking and reinterpretation. To take only one example of the changes wrought by the past twenty years, it is instructive to recall that, as recently as 1971, the biographers of Richardson could solemnly declare of *Clarissa*, "We see very little sex in it, surprisingly little considering the story."[8] From our perspective, it is hard to know what they are talking about: did they believe that only a direct representation of genital acts qualified a work to be about sex? But our surprise at this remark should remind us just how far we have come. On this issue, most of us have now thoroughly internalized the idea that sexuality is not simply a matter of organs and acts but is dispersed through our whole understanding of what it means to be human—law, language, identity, power, and so on. That understanding, in turn, has meant a renewed awareness of the very premises of the fictional art of a writer like Richardson or indeed of the period in general. To put it bluntly, we have nothing to teach these authors about sex. When a writer like Fielding refers to sexual intercourse as so "common and ordinary" that he will not trouble himself with its "particulars" (717, 722), he is not revealing himself to be uninterested in sex, or as a self-importantly chaste narrator; rather, he is reminding us that the act itself is only a small part of that world of thought and feeling and action we call sexual, and that it is that larger world which is his proper narrative pursuit.

But the broadening of our sense of what is "sexual" is only one of the critical changes of the past twenty years, only one of the shifts that has made the eighteenth century "new" again. And sexuality will be only one of the issues that I explore here, for the diversity of recent critical theory means, among other things, that we finally have critical instruments various and flexible enough to match the diversity of the form itself. Now more than ever, we have a range of tools with which to explore the questions and problems that these novels raise. I certainly cannot hope to survey that range of critical possibility, anymore than I can aspire to give a comprehensive reading of these novels or the period in which they appeared. But my attempt here is to make a start, along with all the other beginnings that critics have recently made. Still, criticism is inevitably a matter of beginnings and approaches, not finality or certitude; as so often, Pope's reminder in *The Essay on Criticism* is important:

> . . we tremble to survey
> The growing labours of the lengthened way,
> The increasing prospect tires our wandering eyes,
> Hills peep over hills, and Alps on Alps arise!

1

Robinson Crusoe:
The Eccentric Everyman

Daniel Defoe was not, it seems, a lucky man, suffering as he did the indignities of bankruptcy, the pillory, and Newgate prison; nonetheless, in 1719 he serendipitously invented the English novel. *The Life and Strange Surprizing Adventures of Robinson Crusoe, of York, Mariner* has been accorded this pride of place by many commentators, yet it may strike modern readers as curiously unlike most novels that we know. It claims openly to be allegorical and didactic; it is the story of a life in solitude, devoid of those complications of social life (especially love) which seem to be the genre's primary concern; while realistic in the sense that Defoe pays careful attention to plausibility, it is hopeless with regard to consistency in matters of detail; and it is formally uncertain and shapeless, appearing now as journal, now as a kind of conversational transcript, now as a fully meditated and retrospective autobiography. Why, then, do so many histories of the English novel begin here?[1]

I think the answer lies not with questions of intention, or with subject matter, or with form, but rather with the question of character. Robinson Crusoe, the subject, narrator, and putative author of this "life," is a new kind of hero on the narrative stage, a man who is at once ordinary and exceptional, capable of inspiring broad identification among his readers, yet also clearly individual, even eccentric. In his well-known typology of heroes, Northrop Frye classifies the hero of the novel as "one of us,"[2] a deceptively simple-looking formulation. As many have noted, the novel appears at a time when the very concept of an "individual," of the unique character and destiny of each person, is first coalescing in the Western mind.[3] In such a world, to be "one of us" (not, we note, "*like* us") must imply that what we share, in part, is our very individuality; none of us are alike, and what we have in common is the fact that we are all unique. In the preface to the book, we are told that "the Wonders of this Man's Life exceed all that (he thinks) is to be found extant" (1). The claim insists on Crusoe's exceptional character and yet, significantly, acknowledges the subjectivity of that claim. "He thinks," as we all tend to think, that his life is a story never before told, never to be repeated—in short, a "Wonder."

Frye's phrase, of course, comprehends both the individual and the collective, both "one" and "us," and for all the fact that Crusoe's story is strange and surprising, it is also familiar. Coleridge's is only one among many tributes to Crusoe's place as a kind of everyman: "Crusoe himself is merely a representative of humanity in general; neither his intellectual nor his moral qualities set him above the middle degree of mankind."[4] Crusoe, and the general run of heroes of novels, is thus a paradoxical creature who inspires description by oxymoron—the representative individual, the familiar stranger, the eccentric everyman. (In this regard, it is worth remembering that Pope's *Essay on Man*, which followed *Crusoe* by little more than a decade, also resorts to oxymoron to describe humanity; as the famous lines have it, man is a being "darkly wise and rudely great" [epistle 2, l. 4].) Defoe, in short, created both a memorable character and a remarkably fertile model. What I would like to look at here, then, is Defoe's product. How does Robinson Crusoe, this oxymoronic hero, work?

The immediate source of Crusoe's heroism was the celebrity of Alexander Selkirk, a Scottish sailor who chose to be set down on a deserted island rather than continue a voyage with a captain he disagreed with, and who lived alone on that island for more than four years, until his rescue in 1709. His story is told in several voyaging narratives, and became the subject of a quasi-Rousseauvian account by Richard Steele, who celebrated Selkirk's "untroubled" nights and "joyous" days on his island and drew the predictable moral from the tale, that "he is happiest who confines his Wants to natural Necessities."[5] The fact that Selkirk apparently half-lost his ability to speak did not trouble Steele, whose panegyric on the simple life is, like most of its kind, more innocent by far than its ostensible subject. But how does a real-life celebrity become a fictional hero? As Daniel Boorstin has put it, a celebrity is someone who is famous for being famous;[6] a hero, we feel, must be something more. Why is Crusoe remembered, while Selkirk, whose eighteenth-century equivalent of fifteen minutes of fame has long passed, is preserved only in footnotes and introductions? I think we can approach Crusoe's heroism in two ways, and I want to discuss him in terms of both what he does and what he represents—that is, as both an actor and a symbol, for heroes, if they are to live, are always both.

Paradise Lost, that epic meditation (among other things) on the nature of true heroism, provides us with convenient categories, not only because it examines the issue so profoundly but also because its appearance only fifty years before *Crusoe* signals that shift in thought which makes a character like Crusoe—indeed, perhaps the novel itself—possible.[7] Milton is eager to distinguish between the externalized martial heroism of traditional epic and the internal or spiritual strength ("patience and heroic martyrdom," as he puts it [book 9, ll. 31–32]) of his own new and "more heroic" epic, qualities we see in Adam and Jesus. One effect of Milton's attempt to make a case for an inward heroism is that his poem represents what amounts to a kind of domestic heroism. Ian Watt's characterization of *Paradise Lost* as the "only epic of married life"[8] is typically shrewd. Adam and Eve are heroes because they are capable of mutual forgiveness and because they accept the common woes of labor and pain and death.

In a sense, *Robinson Crusoe* is a sequel to *Paradise Lost*. Milton's epic tells us why survival became both a problem and a duty, and it ends at the point where the struggle to survive begins. Defoe's novel, in turn, picks up the story of that struggle and takes as its fundamental assumption the Miltonic conviction that the apparently humble task of simply living in a fallen world is the truest heroism of all. We must acknowledge, however, that like Milton, Defoe has not wholly abandoned the old heroic model. Milton has Satan, and Crusoe convincingly defeats both cannibal savages and pirates. But those battles occur toward the end of his island exile, and the mariner's primary heroic activity for most of his story is solitary survival, a domestic heroism that I want to examine in some detail.

The extraordinary achievement of Defoe in *Robinson Crusoe* is what we might call the recontextualization of the ordinary, a process that achieves that signal literary virtue of making the familiar strange. Virtually everything that Crusoe does, except live in total isolation for many years, is a mundane activity for someone, at least among those sons of Adam who must labor for a living. Crusoe is, by turns, an architect, a shipwright, a baker, a carpenter, a cook, a farmer, a minister, a potter, a sailor, a salvage man, a shepherd, a surveyor, a tailor—the list could go on, and it would be both comprehensive and quotidian. He is a master of all things everyday. Why, then, is his life so interesting? A chapter title like "Crusoe Makes Bread" (if Defoe had bothered to divide his narrative into smaller units) hardly quickens the pulse or strikes us, under ordinary circumstances, as either "strange" or "surprising." Yet the description of making bread, running about seven pages, does form a kind of chapter and is remarkably compelling.

We are interested in Crusoe's bread for several reasons. As Watt has nicely suggested, the rise of economic specialization in the early modern period created unprecedented new areas on which simple curiosity could fasten itself.[9] To recall the proverb, most people (particularly the middle classes) ceased to be foxes (who know many things) and became instead hedgehogs (who know one big thing), suddenly curious about the activity of all the other specialists around them. Crusoe can say that it is "a little wonderful, and what I believe few People have thought much upon" how many steps are involved in making bread (118) because, for the first time in history, few people in fact did observe or know those procedures. All the tasks Crusoe performs are ordinary to some group, but the vast majority of them were unfamiliar to many of his first or subsequent readers, again especially among the middle classes. Defoe's novel is thus the dim but very real ancestor of all those novels which expose the inner workings of some specialized industry or profession.

Crusoe's comprehensive mastery (or better, his competence: after all, his pots are a bit askew) raises another point about the nature of his heroism. In a notable way, Crusoe can thus represent the same kind of corporate (in the sense of "united in one body") selfhood we often associate with the traditional heroes of epic and romance. We can remember Beowulf, the "good king," who was a comprehensive embodiment of Anglo-Saxon virtues and culture; or we can recall that the individual heroes of the various books of *The Faerie Queene* are only aspects of the corporate hero of the poem, Arthur, who includes them all. Needless to say, Crusoe is not Arthur, whose "magnificence," Spenser tells us, is the sum of all individual virtues. Next to this model, we might see Crusoe's status as the ultimate jack-of-all-trades as merely mock-heroic. I think instead that he reminds us that even heroes who are "one of us" must be exceptional, and that at least part of Crusoe's stature derives from Defoe's ability to make his hero's individual existence include the lives of all those who read his tale. That is, Crusoe as a hero is not only everyman but *all* men, at least all middle-class men, in their very particularity and difference.

But as I have already hinted, the context in which Crusoe's heroic activity takes place is probably even more important than his specific actions—or more precisely, it is the context that makes his activity seem both significant and interesting. As in traditional heroic narrative, the hero's actions take place away from home—at Heorot, in Troy.[10] As the tiresome introductory and concluding episodes of the novel attest (not to mention the stillborn continuations), Robinson Crusoe is the full heroic self that generations have held in their imaginations only on his island. It is the island, we might say, that transforms the everyday into the strange and surprising. Routine is something that tends to turn what is real into a kind of abstraction, and we may lose our sense of self in the role that routine inscribes. Life on the island restores for Crusoe—and vicariously for us the experience of his own activity. Put simply, in this new place Crusoe can see what he is doing. Not that the novel is in any way sensuous. Indeed, *Robinson Crusoe* must be among the least sensuous of fictions and we are always at a loss to know how the bread tasted or whether the goatskin clothing chafed. But the way in which Crusoe, by the power of his own ingenuity (and a small but crucial stock of tools and supplies), single-handedly recapitulates the development of human culture[11]—a good instance of ontogyny repeating phylogyny—recovers each of those activities from the slough of routine. Look again at the bread-making episode.

The obvious analogy of this section of the novel (as well as many others) is to an instructional manual or how-to book, but the perspective is retrospective, not projective, and the unstated title of this episode, as of virtually all episodes in the novel, is not so much "How to Do It" as "How I Did It." We might say that one recipe for a novel is to take an instructional manual and add a hero or heroine. Thus, instead of "How to Handle Sexual Harassment in the Workplace" we get *Pamela* (another contender, we should remember, for "first English novel" and a work that had explicit origins as an advice book). The effect of this combination of hero and how-to is a small narrative that is at once common and singular (as is Crusoe himself). Crusoe makes bread, a process known to many throughout history; but he also makes bread like no one else.

Crusoe's narrative impulse (and this is generally true in Defoe's fiction) is to break up his description of a process into individual steps—hence the resemblance to an instructional manual. Thus, he introduces us to the bread-making adventure by referring to the "strange multitude of little Things necessary in the Providing, Producing, Curing, Dressing, Making, and Finishing this one Article of Bread" (118). We note that word *strange*, repeated from the novel's title, but the steps he ennumerates are peculiar only because humanity has so thoroughly routinized them, which is another way of saying we have forgotten them. The effect of the division of labor within a specialized money economy is to make society as a whole like a cook who can produce a dish without being able to give the recipe. Bread is available, but few of us can say very specifically where it came from. Crusoe makes tangible for us the "strangeness" of the process by reiterating—three times in less than a page—the "multitude of little Things" that produce a loaf of bread. We have already seen one of these lists, but that is not enough for Crusoe; he must also catalog his own ignorance of technique: "I neither knew how to grind or make Meal of my Corn, or indeed how to clean it and part it; nor if Made into Meal, how to make Bread of it, and if how to make it, yet I knew not how to bake it" (117). Moreover, he is compelled to list his material handicaps: "When [the grain] was growing and grown, I have observ'd already, how many things I wanted, to Fence it, Secure it, Mow or Reap it, Cure and Carry it Home, Thrash, Part it from Chaff, and Save it. Then I wanted a Mill to Grind it, Sieves to Dress it, Yeast and Salt to Make it into Bread, and an Oven to Bake it" (118). Crusoe lacks both knowledge and tools, and we watch him as he solves both kinds of problems (always, of course, with "infinite Labour"), tackling and more or less mastering the professions of farmer, potter, stonecutter, miller, and baker along the way.

It is the island that makes all this activity necessary, and it is the island that dictates the way in which Crusoe's technique of bread making will evolve. Processes, no less than species, must evolve in a way that is adapted to the local environment, for if Crusoe's labor here is presented to us under the flag of empiricism, it remains an unrepeatable "Experiment" (123), a compound of ingenuity and persistence, on the one hand, with accident, luck, and compromise, on the other. He may comprehend all the occupations that make bread, but he comprehends them like no other farmer or miller or baker, forced as he is to plant without a plow, grind without stones, and bake without an oven. Certainly there is nostalgia here for a time when labor was, if infinite, still individualized or could be perceived as such. Again, such nostalgia would be especially strong for a middle-class audience, whose lives would have been most altered by economic specialization. But I do not think that the term *nostalgia* really describes what is most powerful in this novel's appeal. Rather, what the island setting accomplishes is to make the ordinary into something that *is* strange and surprising. The setting can do this both because Crusoe has been forced to recover knowledge normally lost in routine and because he must adapt that knowledge to unique local circumstances. A baker is not, in and of himself, a hero, but Crusoe's story reminds us that the first person to bake a loaf of bread must have been a heroic individual.

It would be imprecise to say that heroism in *Robinson Crusoe* is based on the idea that a domestic activity like baking (or building, or carpentry, or goatherding) is as good or important, heroically speaking, as warfare. Rather, Defoe's first novel (and many novels since) creates conditions under which domestic activity becomes something like warfare. When reduced to their barest lineaments, both home life and warfare (at least for the foot soldier) are about survival, but war tends to expose that meaning, whereas domesticity buries the reality of survival beneath comfort and routine. What Defoe's novel recaptures for us is the fact that at the heart of all domestic activity—shelter, food, clothing, the family—is the struggle to survive. This is the knowledge we normally forget, but once the shipwrecked Crusoe registers that he is alive, survival is the very first thing he thinks about: "After I had solac'd my Mind with the comfortable Part of My Condition, I began to look round me . . . and I soon found . . . I had a dreadful Deliverance: For I was wet, had no Clothes to shift me, nor any thing either to eat or drink to comfort me, neither did I see any Prospect before me, but that of perishing with Hunger, or being devoured by wild Beasts" (47). Crusoe's fear is, of course, the truth of the human condition, the wolf that always lurks outside our door and usually outside our consciousness (at least for most Westerners). What Crusoe learns on the island, however, is that humankind really was expelled from Eden, and that in entering the world, we found ourselves in a place where we must labor to survive. Crusoe reliteralizes what

had become—for the middle-class reading public, anyway—merely
a metaphor for human fate. Like Adam, Defoe's hero must earn his
bread in the sweat of his brow. For an ordinary middle-class man,
the recollection that bread and sweat are inextricably linked is often
forgotten, and what *Crusoe* in general is able to accomplish is to
redeem from abstraction and recover for consciousness the truth
that we are all engaged in a literal struggle to survive.

I have said that Robinson Crusoe is a hero not only because of
what he does but also because of what he represents—that he has,
in short, a symbolic value. The foregoing discussion implies part of
what is symbolic about this character: like all heroes—but in a new
way—he becomes a symbol of the universal struggle to maintain
life. But important as that role is in understanding the book's appeal and influence, it does not begin to exhaust Crusoe's symbolic
range, for if heroism is about survival, it is surely also about fantasy, and if we identify with the hero's struggle to live, we also
dream about acquiring his superhuman or exceptional capacities.
In what sense, however, does this homemade and homemaking
hero represent a fantasy? We have seen him as an everyman who
uncovers the heroism of the everyday; how does he also embody
wishes that exceed or escape the human norm?

The fantasies in the novel are legion. For the Protestant reader,
there is the dream of a truly unmediated relationship with God; for
the misanthrope, there is solitude (and for the misogynist, no
women); for the imperialist, there is the natural bounty of a foreign
land with none of the difficulties represented by foreigners. And so
on. But these examples construe the fantasy appeal of *Robinson
Crusoe* too narrowly, for the obverse of the narrative's account of
the struggle to survive is the way it also portrays an almost complete triumph of the will: if, on the one hand, the shipwrecked
Crusoe must honestly confront the pain of the fallen world, he
simultaneously and triumphantly also reenters paradise. Crusoe's
needs and desires are always met, either by the island or by the so-
satisfactory exercise of his own ingenuity. In this regard, his meditation at the end of his fourth year of captivity is worth examination:
"I looked now upon the World as a Thing remote, which I had
nothing to do with, no Expectation from, and indeed no Desires
about. . . . In the first Place, I was removed from all the Wicked-
ness of the World here. I had neither *the Lust of the Flesh, the Lust of
the Eye, or the Pride of Life.* I had nothing to covet; for I had all that I

was now capable of enjoying: I was Lord of the whole Mannor; or if I pleased, I might call myself King, or Emperor. . . . There were no Rivals. I had no Competition" (128). The language has a tincture of religion, including the lines from the Gospel of John, but Crusoe's satisfaction here lies not in any successful rejection of the world, but in his triumph over it.[12] The mariner has that happiness about him known only to those whose victory in the world is complete. Desire indeed is imaged as sin, but we see that sinful desire is the longing for what one cannot have, a species of longing that Crusoe has efficiently exterminated. The apparent simplicity of his claim—that he has what he needs and that he does not want what he cannot have—disguises the kind of omnipotence he has apparently achieved, a power that extends over both the island and his own desiring self.

Crusoe's ability to eliminate inconvenient desire is, of course, a version of that "in-the-world asceticism" which Max Weber attributed to the Protestant mind,[13] but it is finally less important in the novel than the hero's capacity to totalize the very real desires that he does have. When he begins to unload the shipwreck, Crusoe hopes he will find a small inlet stream so that he can land his goods safely. He is not disappointed: "As I imagined, so it was" (51). Here is the existential core of the entire narrative. For all of Defoe's attention to process, to the account of the "infinite Labour" of his hero in accomplishing the simplest task, the novel is most deeply concerned with representing the transformation of the possible or desirable into the actual. The transformations that we watch have an almost-magical power. Crusoe on his island may be, as Watt called him, "economic man,"[14] beavering away at his strange multitude of little tasks, never pausing to examine his protective covering of bourgeois values; but he is also Prospero, master of a transformative magic that can always bend the island to his will—although, appropriately enough for a bourgeois readership, it is a magic without much wonder: a useful definition, perhaps, of technology.

But what *is* Crusoe's will? What does he really want? We have seen various answers already—survival, "serene omnicompetence" (to borrow John Richetti's wonderful phrase),[15] an omnipotence that amounts to a kind of magic. But if we take Crusoe's life on the island as the projection of his interior being, the imaginary made real, what can we say about that interior being, and why have its fantasies served as an expression of the dreams of so many readers?

Psychological realism is an attribute of the novel whose descent is normally traced from an origin in the fictions of Samuel Richardson. And Defoe has often been taken to task both for the absence of any perceptible inner life for his characters (these are people, it is said, of action, not reflection) and for the implausibility of whatever psychology we can discern in them. Psychology, in other words, is something Defoe does either badly or not at all. A good expression of this line of thought was made more than a century ago by Leslie Stephen, who complained that Crusoe behaves like a man "in prison, not in solitary confinement," and that the author gives a "very inadequate picture of the mental torments to which his hero is exposed."[16] Fair enough. But we must make an important distinction here. The character, Robinson Crusoe, may be laughably improbable as a portrait of the psychology of isolation; at the same time, however, he may, as a hero with whom many have identified (including many who have never read the book), tell us a great deal about the psychology of those who find his strange adventures so appealing. That is, a distinction must be drawn between the psychology of the character and the psychology of the kind of heroism he represents. I want to look carefully at the latter question in the discussion that follows. If, as Freud tells us, dreams are the royal road to the unconscious, then Crusoe may be most intriguing if we look at him as a kind of dream. It is a dream that has its origin in the individual writer, Defoe, and it is in many ways peculiar to him; but it is also a dream such as many people have had. Even as an expression of buried fantasies, it appears, Crusoe is an eccentric everyman.

Marthe Robert, in her *Origins of the Novel*, finds in *Robinson Crusoe* an exemplary case of Freud's "family romance," the fantasy that we are not really the children of our parents, but rather have a more glorious origin and are truly the offspring of kings or princes. When Nelly Dean tells Heathcliff in *Wuthering Heights*, "If I were you, I would frame high notions of my birth," she is only carrying coals to Newcastle—according to psychoanalysis, we all fantasize in just that way.[17] At the heart of the fantasy, of course, is a desire to reject one's parents, and the dream of a "romantic" origin reveals itself in the end as the wish to have begotten oneself. Washed up on the island, deprived of any social or familial connection, Crusoe (already a wayward son and the grief of his parents) finds it easy to feel himself not merely reborn but newborn and, in a profound sense, self-generated. The phrase *self-made man* has new significance when applied to Crusoe: in making his "fortune," his island empire, he has also made himself, a new being apparently without reference to any point of origin outside himself. Robert observes that this particular fantasy has proved one of the foundation stones of the novel as a genre, as the long train of fictional orphans that follows Crusoe testifies. Freud's point that even the most terrifying nightmare is actually the fulfillment of a wish seems borne out. But this discussion begs an important question. Why do we fantasize our own orphanage, and—more to the point—why has Crusoe proved so satisfactory an embodiment of that fantasy?

Some nineteenth-century commentators on Defoe, such as Hazlitt and MacCauley, usefully remind us that, in addition to its merits as the first English novel and as a work that has never ceased to survive in the consciousness of the West, *Robinson Crusoe* has always had a special place as a book for boys. "Ever since it was written," Hazlitt writes, it has "excited the first and most powerful influence upon the juvenile mind of England." Rousseau wanted it to be, for a long time, the only volume in his ideal pupil's library.[18] That appeal can certainly be understood without resort to psychoanalysis. Crusoe's island is a kind of ultimate clubhouse, a site of complete independence from adult authority, with no girls allowed. The novel tells the child, especially the male child, that the dependence under which he chafes and which he is already being socialized to reject can be not only lessened but eliminated altogether. You can, *Crusoe* says, stand alone.

Such a reading is useful, but it finally leaves out far too much. Reading *Robinson Crusoe* may have affinities to an Outward Bound expedition, but it is by no means reducible to those terms. To appreciate more fully what the novel suggests about the human condition, we have to come back to the idea of death and especially to the connection between death and the fantasy of self-generation. As Ernest Becker puts it in his reconsideration of the Oedipus complex (which he terms the "Oedipus project"): "The Oedipus project is the flight from passivity, from obliteration, from contingency: the child wants to conquer death by becoming the *father of himself*, the creator and sustainer of his own life" (his italics). The child (which is to say, all of us) sees the very fact of its creation as bearing an irreversible death sentence. That is, birth, copulation, and death are inextricably bound together, and each term always implies the others. To become one's own father, then, is to put oneself in a position to deny the contingent (meaning both dependent and accidental) quality of being. At this point, we can remember Milton's Satan, who tempts the rebel angels to reject their place in a hierarchy of dependence and gratitude with words that epitomize the origin of the fantasy of self-creation: "Remember'st thou / Thy making?" (book 5, ll. 857–58). And the answer to that troubling question is that such knowledge is both what we will never have (an ignorance that makes family romance fantasies possible) and something we must confront constantly (which makes such fantasies necessary).[19] But it is in the denial of his creation that Satan becomes a hero—an inspiring leader, a dauntless warrior, and so on. We have already seen some of the parallels that exist between Crusoe's heroism and that of Adam in *Paradise Lost*, but an equally significant connection exists, in this regard, between Crusoe and Satan. Indeed, there is perhaps a connection between Satan's denial and the nature of heroism itself, conceived in its broadest terms. For Becker, the heroic impulse first manifests itself in the child's desire to be its own parent; that insistence is, as it were, the first strategic maneuver in our lifelong attempt to assert for ourselves a unique value. Heroism consists precisely in that flight from "passivity, obliteration, and contingency" which is the heart of the Oedipus project and which initially appears when we, like the rebel angels, deny the evidence and begin to insist that we made ourselves.

Let us look at these issues more specifically with regard to *Robinson Crusoe*. His story begins in earnest when his own restless nature and the vagaries of tropical sea travel contrive to cast him up on a deserted island, thereby making the fantasy of self-creation more available than usual to realization. In part, the novel works so well because the manifest limitations of Crusoe's situation—no society, no sex, and so on—become the conditions under which this fantasy can flourish, for of course the primary obstacle to the fantasy of self-creation in the real world is otherness: other people in general and, in particular, the others of one's own family, whether parents, mates, or children, those living embodiments of the very cycle of birth and death that we long to escape. When Crusoe says "it was possible for me to be more happy in this forsaken Solitary Condition, than it was probable I should ever have been in any other Particular State in the World" (113), what he implies, in part, is that he has found a setting where his family romance, with himself as his own "Emperor"-father, can proceed without any painful intrusions from that reality principle which other people always represent.

The clearest illustration of this point is provided, however, not by Crusoe's frequent panegyrics on solitude (which, after all, bear at least a passing resemblance to a literary emotion as old as pastoral poetry and which had recently been reexpressed, to take only one example, in Pope's "Ode on Solitude," with its wish to live "unseen, unknown") but by the central dramatic event in the novel: his discovery of the single, naked footprint. It is not, I think, an exaggeration to say that the whole long history of the novel has not produced a more memorable image than the one Crusoe encounters on the day on which he enters, as he says, "a new Scene of my Life" (153).

It happened one Day about Noon going towards my Boat, I was exceedingly surpriz'd with the Print of a Man's naked Foot on the Shore, which was very plain to be seen in the Sand: I stood like one Thunderstruck, or as if I had seen an Apparition; I listen'd, I look'd round me, I could hear nothing, nor could see any Thing; I went up to a rising Ground to look farther, I went up the Shore and down the Shore, but it was all one, I could see no other Impression but that One. . . . [H]ow it came thither, I knew not, nor could in the least imagine. But like innumerable fluttering Thoughts, like a Man perfectly confus'd and out of my self, I came Home to my Fortification, not feeling . . . the Ground I went on, but terrify'd to the last Degree. (153–54)

The dominant note is terror, the terror is of death, and the death he fears, we learn on the next page, is of a particular kind—he sees one footprint and is immediately overwhelmed with the fear that he will be "devoured" by "cannibal Savages" (155). To reduce his psychological reaction to its barest essentials, Crusoe's sudden confrontation with the fact that one other person exists on his island (which is to say, in his world) forces upon him the realization that he can—and of course will—die. The need for his carefully guarded and nurtured fantasy of self-creation is thus exposed: the final meaning of otherness is mortality.

The footprint is an unforgettable image because it metonymically suggests everything that is missing from Crusoe's homemade paradise. As so many readers have noticed, the island is not only unin-habited, it is sexless. Crusoe does not so much as mention women, much less fantasize about an Eve to share his island Eden (and lest we ascribe this absence to some delicacy in Defoe's imagination, we must remember that he went on to write the "memoirs" of the likes of Moll Flanders and Roxanna). But what does "the print of a Man's naked Foot" have to do with sex? Simply this. It is the part that ineluctably implies the whole world of whatever is begotten, born, and dies, the world to which we are all bound. Crusoe's apparently fantastic mental leap from the sight of one foot print to frightened hysteria is only a more vivid image of what we all un-dergo when we recognize the truth about our condition and try to deny the literally mortal implications of our own contingent exis-tence. In a psychologically real sense, Crusoe had in his fifteen years (to this point in the narrative) of solitary self-fashioning won the oedipal battle, become his own father, heroically projected his mastery onto the world. In this light, the footprint is rather like a primal scene, a chilling confrontation with the fact that we are made and did not make ourselves, that we are born to die. The island, which had allowed and nurtured Crusoe's fantasy, is sud-denly reduced to a frame that surrounds one object and one object only—the all-too-legible sign of a footprint. No wonder Crusoe's own feet cannot "feel . . . the ground": he must spurn the island that has betrayed him.

Ortega y Gassett talks about the terror we feel when we truly face the contingent reality of the human condition. His remarks are apt, in large part because of what they say about what is missing from the psychological world of *Robinson Crusoe*, what makes it *un*realistic: "And this is the simple truth—that to live is to feel oneself lost—and he who accepts it has already begun to find him-self, to be on firm ground. Instinctively, as do the shipwrecked, he will look round for something to which to cling, and that tragic, ruthless glance . . . will cause him to bring order to the chaos of his life. These are the only genuine ideas; the ideas of the ship-wrecked."[20] Ortega's point here parallels the one made above: the problem of survival is one we can normally repress, and "the ship-wrecked" man is, for him, the person who has stripped the prob-lem of its film of narcotic familiarity. But Crusoe, except for a rare moment like his discovery of the footprint, enjoys a preposterous triumph, and the fact that he is literally shipwrecked never really brings him to a sense of the inevitable compromise we must make with reality (that "something to which to cling" that Ortega speaks of) and its limitations. The encounter with otherness that begins with the footprint, far from permanently altering the sense of mastery that Crusoe has acquired because of his isolation, is only a temporary setback, and becomes instead the occasion for new triumphs. In time, he will master the cannibals, and Friday, and the mutinous crew, just as he had already mastered bread. From a fantasy of self-creation we proceed to a fantasy of social control, and Crusoe, who initially proves he can stand alone, ultimately proves he can stand first. The encounter with otherness, far from being a harbinger of mortality or of any tragic compromise, becomes instead the occasion of another victory, another magic transformation of the stuff of imagination into a tangible world.

I am not concerned in this study to work out, in a programmatic way, *Robinson Crusoe* as the expression or illustration of any school of psychoanalysis. Certainly the novel offers rich soil for those interested in that kind of harvest, and we could go on to explore more fully, for example, the connection between Crusoe's assumption that the footprint belongs to a cannibal and the insecure ego's fear of sexuality as a form of engulfment in which it can be destroyed. Eating and sexuality have been associated in the human psyche time out of mind, and to say that there is "no sex" in *Robinson Crusoe* is only to say that the sexuality is displaced or rechanneled in typical ways. What I am most concerned about is an understanding of the kind of heroism that Robinson Crusoe represents, and I believe that psychoanalysis offers some help in describing certain aspects of Crusoe's heroic appeal.

As I noted before, *Robinson Crusoe* is far more interesting for what it can tell us about the psychology of heroism than for what it knows about the psychology of its hero. We must also acknowledge, however, that this peculiar and improbable figure, Robinson Crusoe, proved an exceptionally fertile model for later artists in the newborn tradition of the novel to follow. To return to my original point of departure, I think that Crusoe became so fruitful a pattern because it was Defoe's genius to create a character who was at once exceptional and ordinary. To recall Frye's phrase, Crusoe is "one of us," both an individual and a focus for broad identification. Such a combination, in turn, becomes one source of the wide appeal of novels in general; that mixture, however, can take several forms. In *Crusoe* we have a rather average man placed in an unprecedented setting, one that allows Defoe to achieve an exceptional realization of quite-ordinary fantasies—of mastery and immortality. In the "Prelude" to *Middlemarch*, George Eliot reminds us of another way these elements may be combined, when she describes those "many Theresas . . . who found for themselves no epic life wherein there was a constant unfolding of far-resonant action; perhaps only a life of mistakes, the offspring of a certain spiritual grandeur ill-matched with the meanness of opportunity."[21] Here we have a kind of inversion of Defoe's formula; instead of an ordinary man thrust into extraordinary circumstances, we have exceptional women trapped by the "meanness" of heroic opportunity. As we will see, that particular kind of dissonance marks characters as disparate as Richardson's Lovelace and Austen's Emma. But both formulas have been played out in thousands of novels, all of which, I would say, owe a debt to Daniel Defoe, so luckless and yet so prescient, who hit upon the idea of this mariner, the eccentric everyman. Perhaps the debt should be owed to Milton and the domestic heroism of Adam and Eve. But the splendor and sublimity of *Paradise Lost* proved more of an obstacle to later creation than a pattern for imitation. Instead, a usable pattern was first sketched by Defoe. His product is as rough cut as Crusoe's own clothes or furniture. But Defoe's standard, like that of his hero, is not perfection but utility, and a large part of what Crusoe represents for posterity is a model of heroism that *worked*. His name is legion.

2

Clarissa:
The Power of a Name

The Question of Editions

Editorial questions and problems rarely intrude on the experience of the common reader and, in today's interpretative climate, are often of little concern to most scholars and critics. *Clarissa*, however, is a special case, perhaps even a unique one, and for several reasons. First, the "complete" text (a problematic concept, as we will see) is prodigiously long. By whatever *Guinness* book standard one wishes to apply (words, pages), it is the longest novel in the language, a mountain of paper that has become especially daunting to modern audiences. Moreover, Samuel Richardson was not content to let stand the text he published in three installments between 1747 and 1748. In large part because of audience disagreements about Lovelace's character and the book's tragic conclusion, Richardson embarked on a series of revisions that ultimately added two hundred pages to the text and that saw the addition of badgering footnotes (a typical one begins, "The careful reader will have noted . . ."), a new preface, an afterword, and a descriptive index of the letters. Richardson's goal in all this was simple and impossible: to ensure that reader response exactly matched authorial intent.

As a result, the modern reader of *Clarissa* has three choices of texts. He or she can approach the novel through John Butt's 1932 edition, which generally follows the third edition (1751) and incorporates Richardson's additions, notes, and tendentious framing devices; through Angus Ross's 1985 text, which closely matches the first edition and thus omits the additions; or through what has probably been the most popular classroom text, George Sherburn's 1962 abridgment, based on Butt's edition, which compresses the mammoth narrative into something like a third its original length.[1] Beginning with Richardson himself, many have believed that the choice of edition makes an enormous difference in the meaning of the novel. Richardson obviously thought that the moral he in-

21

tended was insufficiently clear in the first edition; his revisions thus validate the later editions as truer to his intent. On the other hand, a modern critic like W. B. Warner, who is committed to an interpretive stance that frees the text from authorial control, commends the first edition as truer to the novel's own possibilities, which he believes Richardson himself had no privileged command over. Further, Warner insists that Sherburn's abridgment is itself an interpretive statement, one that is biased in favor of Clarissa and against Lovelace.[2]

Warner's arguments are powerful, and yet my own experience of reading and teaching the various versions of the novel suggests to me that the textual/editorial problem, for all its fascination, may in many ways be irrelevant. *Clarissa* is interesting in part because of its refusal to validate finally any interpretive position, and this magnificent fiction somehow survives all attempts—by abridgers, editors, and even its own author—to fix it, either as a text or as a moral statement. The remarkable experience of reading the book, especially its peculiar power to disturb, is somehow immanent in whatever version we take up.

This independence of the story from the text (to adopt a simple distinction) has been the subject of a great deal of the recent commentary on *Clarissa*, especially Warner's book; I would like to suggest three textual reasons here. First, absurd as it may seem in the face of the novel's length, there is a way in which *Clarissa* always makes us feel that any version of it is already abridged. Most fictions rely on a kind of persistence of vision. Any narrative has its gaps, but especially in fictions that strive to achieve the illusion of realism, we tend to elide those gaps in much the same way as we visually compose the individual frames of a film into a seamless whole. In *Clarissa*, the seams are always showing. This fact is in part an effect of the epistolary form: the novel consists not just of letters but of *many* letters, and at the end of each of them we are made aware, in the crudest typographical way, of the white space on the page—literal gaps in the story that the next letter can never quite fill in. Second, even the longest edition of the novel refers to letters that we never see, most significantly the correspondence of Clarissa and Lovelace while she is still at Harlowe Place. In other words, any version of the novel is already only a selection of the letters these characters are supposed to have written. Finally, letters in *Clarissa*, unlike those in *Pamela*, have a kind of accordion effect. They tend to expand to include other writing, so that any individual letter may contain copies of other letters sent to or received from correspondents other than the one addressed, legal documents such as wills, and so on. For example, letter 29 of volume 1, addressed to Anna Howe, contains letters from Clarissa to her brother and her sister and each of their replies, in addition to what Clarissa says to Miss Howe—five letters in all. In revising the novel, Richardson added only seven new letters; primarily, he added new material to letters already there.[3] Conversely, abridgers rarely eliminate whole letters but instead compress. Each letter thus becomes like one moment of the footrace in Zeno's paradox—infinitely dividable into more and more minute examinations of the flux and reflux of consciousness. Theoretically, it seems, one letter could expand infinitely. The effect is to leave the reader suspicious that no end can be reached, no complete record of the mind's activity achieved. We can only dip into the stream of consciousness, and in this, the longest of novels, we always feel as if what we have is an approximation of the events narrated—a truth about all narrative but one that *Clarissa* brings uncomfortably home.

The Novel

If the telling of Clarissa's story is long, the plot itself is simple—and brutal. *Clarissa* is punctuated by acts of violence (the rape, the duels that open and close the book) and by images of force (the reddening print of James Harlowe's hand on Clarissa's arm, Clarissa fending off Lovelace by a penknife held to her breast). Long before the heyday of Victorian melodrama, Clarissa on several occasions utters the melodramatist's favorite words, "Unhand me, Sir!" Yet these physical manifestations are rare, so rare as to be greeted almost with relief when they do occur. But physical violence is only a symptom of a larger, more pervasive issue: power. *Clarissa* is obsessed with power, but power as exercised emotionally, psychologically, and morally, and with words—spoken or written—as the usual tools by which power is enforced. The power struggles are played out on a number of fronts. There is always the contention of gender, the struggle by each sex to know and, by knowing, overpower the other. Lovelace and Clarissa are the central antagonists here, but virtually every relationship in the novel—including that between Clarissa and the male Harlowes and that between Lovelace and the whores—is colored by the battle of sexual difference. There is also the battle within families, either between generations or between siblings. And finally, underlying all the struggles between people, there is the struggle within the self—to know it and, for some, to control what seems like the frightening chaos of the inner life.

What is ostensibly at stake in almost every power struggle in the novel is Clarissa's virginity. Who has the disposal of what Fielding referred to as "a poor girl's little, etc."?[4] Will it be the Harlowes, who wish to marry her off to "rich Solmes," a loathsome toady who appears to combine the worst aspects of impotence and sadism? Will it be Lovelace, obsessed with the idea of bringing "virtue to a trial," of discovering whether Clarissa's "frost be frost indeed"? Or will the heroine achieve her cherished "single life"? Everyone in the novel has something crucial at stake in Clarissa's maidenhead. For the Harlowes, apparently, it is money; for Lovelace, it seems, the wager is more intellectual: what is the nature of female virtue? and for Clarissa, the issue is no less than that of selfhood, for she has invested the integrity of her identity in the intactness of her body. If we look at each of these struggles in more detail, however, we see that the issue of virginity is more complicated than this brief statement of competing motivations would suggest. And if we step back even further, we must ask what is at stake in this battle for Richardson himself and his first, rapt readers? To keep the discussion that follows as clear as possible, I will for the most part talk about the main actors in the novel independently of these last questions. The problem of the relation between these actors and both their author and their audience will then be the focus of this chapter's conclusion.

First, the long family war at Harlowe Place. As early as the preface to the first installment of the first edition, Richardson had claimed that "one of the principal views" he had in publishing the novel was "to caution parents against the undue exercise of their natural authority over their children in the great article of marriage" (Ross, 36). The question then arises, In what way is the Harlowes' attempt to exercise their authority "undue"? Many critics have been satisfied to explain their excesses as the sin of greed.[5] The Harlowes are rich, but they want to be richer and they want a title for their eldest son, James; Solmes wants Clarissa and offers marriage settlements that flatter their fondest ambitions. Clarissa is thus caught between the avarice and ambition of her family and Solmes's desire for the neighborhood paragon.

Such an arrangement, of course, is called property marriage, and the key piece of property in the transaction is Clarissa herself. But in what way do daughters represent property? According to many anthropologists, most prominently in recent years Claude Lévi-Strauss, society itself (or culture) originates in a system of exchange whereby families give up their own daughters in order that their sons, in turn, may marry the daughters given up by other families. That is, an incest taboo and the consequent necessity to marry outside the family create a system of exchange between families that in turn becomes the basis of that web of mutual obligation we call society.[6] In these terms, what the Harlowes are proposing is a property marriage that apparently fits this model perfectly: in exchange for Clarissa, one piece of property, they receive settlements of land and money from Solmes.

A number of readers, the historian Christopher Hill most prominently, have argued that *Clarissa* represents an extended protest against property marriages.[7] Opposition to such marriages was indeed commonplace in mid-eighteenth-century England, but I am not sure that we should see *Clarissa's* depiction of parent-child relations as in any way commonplace. By any measure, the doings at Harlowe Place are very strange. The family certainly does want to exercise "undue" authority over their youngest daughter, but their real ambition is to subvert the system of exchange, not uphold or use it. James, in a statement that begins to suggest his typical brutality, bitterly condemns the exchange system: "Daughters," he says, "are chickens brought up for the tables of other men" (1:54). In keeping with his attitude here, the proposed marriage with Solmes proves, on close examination, only a mirage of exchange. The Harlowes' real intention is to keep this most valuable piece of property, Clarissa, to themselves. In a speech that is exemplary for the plot of many English novels, Clarissa describes with considerable poignancy what it feels like for a young girl in her late teens to face marriage: "*Marriage* is a very solemn engagement, enough to make a young creature's heart ache, with the *best* prospects, when she thinks seriously of it! To be given up to a strange man; to be ingrafted into a strange family; to give up her very name . . . ; to be obliged to prefer this strange man, to father, mother—to everybody" (1: 152–53). But will she really be "given up"? I think not. If we look at any of the elements in this exchange—the settlements, the ceremony, the life Clarissa will supposedly be engrafted onto, and above all the groom, the "odious Solmes" himself—what we will see is that the Harlowes are giving up nothing.

Although Clarissa's great fear here is the loss of the family she has always known, what is curious about the opening section of the novel, which describes the attempt to force the Solmes match, is the way everything she fears most occurs *before* the wedding. As soon as she makes her resistance to Solmes clear, James informs Clarissa that she may not see her parents: "MISS CLARY,—By command of your father and mother I write expressly to forbid you to come into their presence or into the garden when *they* are there" (1: 114). Marriage to Solmes is presented as the way to *restore* family ties: "*Then it would be all well. . . . Then they should dote upon me. . . . Love me as well as ever*" (1: 31). She becomes a prisoner in her own room, is isolated from her family and friends, and is forced to communicate by surreptitious letters and through the vindictive mediation of her siblings and their servants. The Harlowes' plans for the wedding ceremony underline this reversal with a transparent bit of spatial symbolism. Instead of being given away by her father in the traditional way, Clarissa will be reunited with her parents after the ceremony. They will not see her, it seems, "till all was over, and till they had a good account of [her] behavior" (1: 426). As her aunt describes the aftermath of such a wedding, the picture is not one of transition, of engrafting onto a new family, but one of a return: "[H]ow joyful it would be . . . to see my father, my mother, my uncles, my brother, my sister, all embracing me with raptures, . . . and congratulating each other on their restored happiness" (1: 469). The significant word here is *restored,* and in the moment of nuptial bliss it is the Harlowes themselves who do the embracing. The groom is left quite out.

That brings us to Solmes, an unpolished arriviste and, according to Clarissa, bent, "broad-shouldered," and splayfooted (1: 78–79). What part does he play in the Harlowe dream of power? Clarissa seems to be quite afraid of him; she calls him a "monster" (1: 79) and says his face "seems formed to express" anger (1: 400). Anna Howe reports that the proposed groom has said that "fear and terror . . . looked pretty in a bride as well as in a wife" (1: 284). But for a monster, Solmes is oddly ineffectual, and it is quickly apparent to us, if not to Clarissa, that he is the Harlowes' pawn, one they will discard as soon as his usefulness is over. This point is most powerfully represented in one of the novel's great dramatic scenes, the formal courtship visit Solmes pays Clarissa shortly before she elopes. Ostensibly, Solmes will read a letter to Clarissa (one that will make her ears "tingle" [1: 305]) describing some of Lovelace's more lurid sexual crimes. The real force of the scene, however, is the power struggle between Clarissa and her family. As her uncle tells Solmes, "She must, she shall . . . be yours. We'll see who'll conquer, parents or child" (1: 393). Solmes is merely the site where the battle takes place.

Solmes's subordinate role in this family drama is emphasized by the fact that Clarissa will not even have to consummate the marriage. "Mr. Solmes," her aunt assures her, "will be under an engagement . . . after the ceremony is past, . . . to leave you at your father's, and return to his own house every evening, until you are brought to a full sense of your duty" (1: 440). One rubric of the "noble" settlements Solmes has offered, however, suggests that the Harlowes can wait a long time for their once-and-future daughter to realize her "duty." Clarissa's own estate, her beloved Dairy House that her grandfather willed to her and that is the ground of so much contention, will revert to the Harlowes only if her marriage to Solmes is barren. We can see in such reversionary dreams a powerful emblem for the Harlowes' whole enterprise in arranging the Solmes match. The Dairy House becomes a kind of self-dowry: before she can (re)enter a family, Clarissa, like other brides in the exchange system, must give something to the group she is (re)joining. As with the rest of the marriage arrangements with Solmes, there is an illusion of exchange created but all the movements—of property and of person—remain internal to the Harlowes.

Eventually, Clarissa recognizes the situation for what it is and sees marriage to Solmes as being "delivered over to my brother" (1: 32). In that light, the monstrosity of Solmes is not so much the pecuniary greed he represents but another form of avarice: incest. The Harlowes appear to be passionately afraid of losing this property, either to Lovelace—whose ancient family reminds them of their upstart class status, just as his confident manhood underlines their sexual inadequacies—or to her own independence. In a revealing moment, shortly after the Solmes interview, Clarissa overhears James exulting to Bella, "Now must she be what we would have her be" (1: 430). As we will see, Clarissa threatens them precisely because she holds the promise that she will not have to "be" a Harlowe, and their only scheme for keeping her is this strange and violent compulsion to marry her off to Solmes, a man (as Clarissa says) without bowels, without self-respect, who exists to be used and discarded. If the foundation of patriarchal power rests on the system of exchange of women, then the Harlowes attempt to take that power one step further—their power will lie not in engineering exchange but in refusing it.[8]

The power Lovelace longs to exercise is more intellectual but, as we have too often been reminded in human history, no less brutal for that. Lovelace has a bad reputation among many critics for what one of them has termed his "uncensored appetites," but Lovelace is being quite honest when he describes himself as "no sensual man" (2: 147).[9] For him, pleasure resides in the game of seduction, not the conclusion; as he says, "What . . . is the enjoyment of the finest woman in the world, to the contrivance, the bustle, the surprises, and at last the happy conclusion of a well-laid plot. . . . [T]he doubts; the apprehensions; the heartachings, the meditated triumphs—these are the joys that make the blessing dear. For all the rest, what is it?" (3: 248). When Anna Howe tells Clarissa that Lovelace retires every night with his "pen in his fingers" (1: 49), the innuendo only reinforces our sense of what this man's real sexual organ is.

Lovelace is, as one commentator has put it, "Richardson's extravagant triumph."[10] He is a triumph because he is not reducible to the kind of morality-play vice figure Richardson seems at times to have believed he had created. At one point, Lovelace pleads with Belford, "Do not despise me, Jack, for my inconsistency—in no two letters perhaps agreeing with myself" (2: 460). Indeed, he plays many roles in this work he so often dominates: he is a "plotting fellow," the gleeful breaker of a hundred maidenheads, whose main concern is the reputation he will have in "rakish annals"; but he is also an intellectual libertine very much in the spirit of Sade, one who believes that sex is fundamentally criminal and that its criminality is to be emphasized by the elaborate staging of sexual crime. Often, Lovelace is merely a spokesman for his time, and as we will see, he is filled with and controlled by conventional wisdom about female identity; here is the man who boasts, "Don't I know the sex?" (2: 209). But he protests too much. In perhaps more important ways, Lovelace is a troubled and very troubling questioner of just those assumptions, a man who wonders deeply what it means to be born woman, who is obsessed with discovering whether gender is biological nature or cultural construction. Here we find Lovelace at both his most attractive, as he tries to see through rather than with cultural categories, and his worst, as when he, like some Nazi doctor, tries to mask sadistic urges behind the cool stance of a scientist, one who can claim that "my principal design is but to bring virtue to a trial" (2: 325).

From the novel's first appearance, Richardson had said that one of his primary motives in writing *Clarissa* was to warn "children" (by which he seems to mean "marriageable women") against "preferring a man of pleasure to a man of probity upon the dangerous but too commonly received notion, *that a reformed rake makes the best husband*" (Ross, 36). Since this idea lies so importantly behind the conception of Lovelace's character, it is worth pausing to examine it. Why did people in that age think a reformed rake made the best husband? And what kind of a rake is Lovelace?

Certainly, the doctrine of the reformed rake had wide literary currency: reclaimed libertines frequented the late Restoration stage, and in the early novel there are many characters—like Wilson in *Joseph Andrews* and Dennison in Smollet's *Humphry Clinker*—who fit the type. Tom Jones is perhaps the fullest exploration and, I would say, affirmation of the idea, but the belief also animates (for all his protests in *Clarissa*) Richardson's own first novel: *Pamela*'s Mr. B is nothing if not a rake who becomes a good husband. The notion of the reformed rake is the eighteenth-century manifestation of that ancient double standard which winked at male promiscuity while insisting on female fidelity, and we can see the way the era elaborated the doctrine as a way to socialize and control traditional male sexual license and to do so in a way that manages to flatter both male and female vanity. Look at the way Mandeville describes the idea: "The experienced Man . . . has try'd several Women; he finds they all agree in one Particular, and that after a Storm of Love there always succeeds a Calm: When he enters into Matrimony, he is prepared against any Disappointments of that Nature, and is ready to make Allowance for those Faults and Imperfections which are inseparable from Human Kind. This is so true, that Women have established a Maxim, that Rakes make the best husbands."[11] As Blake put it later, the road of excess leads to the palace of wisdom, or at least to the palace of a good marriage. In keeping with the age's fundamental empiricism, the rake experiments, learns the truth about women and himself, and then settles down, and the institution of marriage is stronger for it. Male vanity is clearly flattered: men can continue to reserve for themselves the privilege of sexual experience and rationalize it as education. But such education is not only for themselves. Mandeville says that women themselves have established the maxim, and Lovelace will echo him: "Now women, Jack, like not novices. . . . They are pleased with a love of the sex that is founded in the *knowledge of it*" (3: 81).

The fact that the doctrine justifies male license is not, however, the only way in which it is flattering. If men entering marriage carry the power of their sexual experience, the women whom they marry are ostensibly the agents of the reform—it is at their feet that these lions will lie down, renouncing vice for life with a good woman. As Anna Howe, who has no rake of her own and who often seems to long for one, reminds Clarissa, "[W]ho knows not that love delights in taming the lion-hearted?" (1: 243). We could even see the nuptial pair as structurally equivalent, for the reverse side of the "experienced Man" is the virgin bride, and if a reformed rake makes the best husband then we have to remember that the age believed that a reformed virgin makes the best wife. Each gives up a sexual identity that is essentially individual and socially threatening (promiscuity attacks social cohesion; chastity, social existence) for one that is socially affirmative. Rakes and virgins give up the dangerous isolation of lust and purity and re-form to become husbands and wives, component parts of that microcosm of social order, the family.

While Lovelace adores adopting the posture of the reformable rake, he is at heart as suspicious of the doctrine as his creator. And his suspicions become clearest when we look at the nature of the "trial" to which he subjects Clarissa. What he has embarked on is an attempt to see "if her frost be frost indeed." But what does he mean by *frost?*

Lovelace wants to know if virginity deserves the name his age has given it: virtue. At times, he shows himself curious about this question for the most conventional of reasons. The historian Keith Thomas has argued that the traditional insistence on the virginity of a bride is rooted in her value as property in the exchange system already described.[12] A man's exclusive control of his wife's virginity is not a moral issue but a financial one: it proves that he owns her. Such a belief was widespread in the eighteenth century, especially as it related to questions of inheritance. Dr. Johnson remarked several times that "upon [female chastity] all the property in the world depends."[13] Lovelace seconds this conviction often, as when he states, "[T]he wife, by a failure [of chastity], may do much more injury to the husband than the husband can do to the wife . . . by obtruding another man's children into his possessions" (2: 39).

Lovelace, however, is considerably more than his own private detective, engaged in a routine background check. For all his braggart claims to "know the Sex," he is deeply perplexed about female identity in general and Clarissa's in particular. It is a very primitive and powerful impulse to believe that morality is bodied forth, to hope that the body is a text on which we can read the soul. "Anatomize Regan," says Lear. "See what breeds about her heart." Lovelace wants to know if virginity and virtue really are connected, to find out if the equation between a physical condition and a moral state is conventional and arbitrary or if it is ontological. Appropriately enough for a man whose mind is uncertain, Lovelace has many theories about the nature of women's virtue. Early on, he says, "Pride is perhaps the principal bulwark of female virtue" (2: 36). Note the *perhaps*; perhaps, however, it is education: "Do not their grandmothers give them one easy rule?—Men are to ask; women are to deny" (2: 185). But this is an interrogative; moreover, what does *no* mean if women always say it? And if virginity *is* virtue, what happens when virginity is lost? Does the body change if its embodied moral center is taken away? Lovelace seems to believe that it does; as his own "rake's creed" has it, *"Once subdued, . . . always subdued"* (3: 190). But what is "subdued"? Is it the triumph of nature over culture, the release of sexual feelings long repressed? Is it the triumph of masculine over feminine "pride"? In the terms of the property model, does it mean simply that the owner has taken possession of his stock? Or is it a triumph of the will, one person's power proved stronger than the other's?

It is in light of this confusion that we must examine the central event of this long novel—Lovelace's rape of the drugged and unconscious Clarissa. It is a bizarre event in every way, and the strangest thing about it is that it happens at all. Lovelace has said that he is no sensual man, a point he emphasizes often: "More truly delightful to me the seduction progress than the crowning act: for

that's a vapour, a bubble!" (2: 337). And he has vigorously dismissed rape: "Abhorred be *force*, be the *necessity* of force, if that can
be avoided! There's no triumph in *force*. No conquest over the
will. . . . *Force* is the devil!" (2: 398). Yet he does rape Clarissa, rape
her after deceiving and drugging her, and apparently in view of the
"old dragon," Mrs. Sinclair, and her myrmidon whores. The man
who loves the "seduction" progress has resorted to its demonic
double, rape,[14] and the question must be, Why? What does he
hope to learn or achieve by sexual intercourse with an unconscious
virgin whom he claims to love?

Shortly before the "black transaction," Lovelace tries to explain
his intentions to Belford: "Is not *this* the hour of her trial—and in
her, of the trial of the virtue of her whole sex, so long premeditated,
so long threatened? Whether her frost be frost indeed? Whether
her virtue be principle? Whether, if *once subdued, she will not be
always subdued?* And will she not want the very crown of her
glory . . . if I stopped short of the ultimate trial?" (3: 190). It is
curious to consider what kind of "evidence" an unconscious witness could give. Lovelace speaks of the rape as a trial of her manner
(her "frost"), of her "virtue" (whether it is "principle" or merely
policy), and of her will—which is to say that it is a test of her body
as a text of her soul, and Lovelace wants to know if he can change
what her body says. His assumption here is apparently dualistic:
that the body, when separated from the mind (the source of manners, of policy), will confirm itself as essentially animal. Lovelace is
fond of quoting Pope's judgment, "Ev'ry woman is at heart a rake,"
and the rape seems to be his method of getting at the physical truth
of Clarissa and, through her, all women. Is "the Sex" sexual or not?

Lovelace is not sure. He repeatedly insists that the rape—indeed,
his whole "courtship" of Clarissa—is a trial, an experiment. Perhaps he is wrong, perhaps virtue is principle, perhaps frost is not
merely a convention. That possibility, however, raises another set
of questions, questions that suggest Lovelace's peculiarity. Why
does he care so much? Why go to these lengths to discover what
other men seem not to have much worried about, whether women
are "naturally" virtuous or carnal?

I suspect that the answer lies in Lovelace's claim to be "no sensual man." Shortly after the rape, he claims that the "enjoyment of
the finest woman in the world" leads only to the discovery that "an
angel in imagination [has] dwindled down to a woman in fact" (3:

248). On one level, the rape is an attempt to see whether a woman incapable by way of unconsciousness of playing the *role* of "angel," one who has been reduced to pure flesh, can still *be* an angel or whether she too will prove only "a woman in fact." What is clear is that Lovelace—and this begins to make him look like a very odd rake indeed—does not want what he calls a "woman." Belford, the rake who does reform, describes the libertine like this:

> What woman, nice in her person, and of purity in her mind and manners, did she know what miry wallowers the generality of men of our class [gentleman rakes] are in themselves, and constantly trough and sty with, but would detest the thoughts of associating with such filthy sensualists, whose favourite taste carries them to mingle with the dregs of stews, brothels, and common sewers?
>
> Yet, to such a choice are many worthy women betrayed, by that false and inconsiderate notion, raised and propagated, no doubt, by the author of all delusion, *that a reformed rake makes the best husband.* (4: 389)

The language here is straight from the mourner's bench, and Belford's self-loathing (after all, he was a miry wallower himself) is that which converts often feel for the life they have left behind. Rakes, he says, are filthy sensualists and must seek women who mirror their taste; by definition, it seems, no woman who could feel such desire is worthy to be a wife. But Belford's comments have nothing to do with Lovelace's taste in these matters. Lovelace is no sensualist, and he rejects women who have been sexualized, "women in fact." As he says, "O Jack! What devils are women, when all tests are got over, and we have completely ruined them!" (3: 430). The assumption, here anyway, is clear: virtue is a facade, women are really devils, and the truth emerges through the "test." In this mood, Lovelace parodies the empiricism that his age valued so strongly.

But Lovelace is the scientist as sadist and as megalomaniac. The purpose of the test is less to discover the truth than to confirm his control, to prove himself to himself once more. The kind of power Lovelace desires must be described very carefully, for it is easy to see it as traditional, as a manifestation of a patriarchal need to ensure the dependence of women, to insist on their subservience within a system dominated by men. His demand that Clarissa acknowledge his power, his refusal to allow her any escape—

intellectual, emotional, or physical—from his grasp, can certainly be read as a microcosmic playing out of the prevailing social structure. We remember, too, Brownmiller's point: the fear of rape is the way all men keep all women under control.[15] But just as the Harlowes reveal themselves as subversive of the norm they apparently uphold, so does Lovelace. He, too, seeks a power that is essentially disruptive.

Let's look further at the rape. Before an earlier attempt to take Clarissa by surprise, the fire scene, Lovelace had explained his strategy thus: "I may do what I will, and plead for excuse violence of *passion*" (2: 471). "Violence of passion" is thus revealed as artifice, and such a desire to remake the physical into the intellectual is, in miniature, Lovelace's attitude toward his own sexuality. We have already seen his love of "the seduction progress" and his dismissal of "the end." The rape of Clarissa is fiction's most memorable expression of sexual contempt, not only because it shows hatred for the body of the female other but also because of the hatred it shows for his own. As we know, rape is a crime of violence, not of uncontrollable eros, but Lovelace has refined the sexlessness of rape even further. The rape is public, performed with the collusion of the whores and in their presence, thus emphasizing that Lovelace is constructing a scene with an audience rather than indulging an impulse, even a violent one. The potential physical passion of resistance has been eliminated by drugs. It's all rather like a surgical demonstration performed in an operating theater. Now that the "end" has arrived, Lovelace has dismissed all "charming roundabouts" (3: 248) and has constructed consummation in such a way as to reduce or eliminate anything, be it pleasure or pain, that might serve to remind him that he is flesh and blood. As we saw with Crusoe and the footprint, the confrontation with otherness is always a reminder of the contingency of our own existence, and Lovelace in a profound way has tried to guarantee that there is no other there. The act may be, as Shakespeare's Troilus has it, a slave to limit, but Lovelace has tried to demonstrate his power over the inherent limitations of physical existence by reducing the act even further, to a point, sexually speaking, near absolute zero. No wonder his report of the rape is the shortest letter in the novel.

In other words, Lovelace has constructed this scene so that he never loses himself in the actions of his own or another body. His flesh is reduced to a kind of purely instrumental role—his consciousness rules at all times. And Clarissa has been brought down to the level of flesh without consciousness—that is, a body that is also completely subservient to his will. Belford has said that she seemed to him to be "all mind" (2: 243), but here, consciousness removed, she has become just a body. It is this necrophiliac aspect of the rape that reverses the typical critical division of these characters into a fleshly Lovelace and a spiritual Clarissa.[16] The rape *is* dualistic but in the opposite way: Lovelace-as-consciousness rapes Clarissa-as-flesh. In his very first letter, Lovelace has said that he "hate[d]" love "because 'tis my master" (1: 152), and here he tries to demonstrate his mastery—and his mastery through contempt—of that god. He hates the body, and when he finally has sex (the only act of sexual intercourse in all of Richardson's sexually charged fiction that we know of directly), he designs the action as an expression of contempt for sex itself. Lovelace too wants to be "all mind."

A rake like Belford (or Wilson, or Dennison, or Tom Jones) is part of the social system of gender relations as the age constituted them. These men sow wild oats with "fallen" women, to some degree they "reform," and they marry virgins. The double standard preserves both male license and male property, guaranteeing men pleasure and power. In light of this system, Lovelace looks very strange. One essential component of the double standard is that any fallen woman is every man's fair game (Molly Seagrim in *Tom Jones* comes to mind), whereas a virgin should be approached honorably. For Belford, this principle means that the "work of bodies" (by which he seems to mean sexual pleasure) should be left to "mere bodies" (2: 244). Lovelace will have nothing to do with this attitude. His own "rake's creed" states, "*Once any other man's, . . . and never more mine*" (2: 428), and he dismisses the pursuit of "mere bodies" as "the palliating consolation of a Hottentot heart, determined . . . to gluttonize on the garbage of other foul feeders" (2: 327). Such a philosophy of the bedroom justifies his affection for the "seduction progress," of course, but the real implications are much darker. In a culture like his own that demanded that unmarried women hide their sexual feelings, Lovelace's pursuit of virgins ensures that his sexual world will be one in which power, not physical pleasure, is dominant. Lovelace thus wants power over himself and the other person, but he also wants it over society itself. By debauching virgins and turning them into "devils," Lovelace erodes the whole system—and not with an eye to the "liberation" of an oppressed group. In the end, Lovelace's motives are too complex to forge into unity. As a social rebel, he is a man who often appears to be asking a question well worth asking: how has culture constructed gender? But he is also a kind of megalomaniac, determined to burrow under the foundation of that system not because it is bad but so that the glory of its destruction will elevate him as a kind of Samson in the hall of rakish fame.

As Warner has pointed out, the history of criticism regarding *Clarissa* seems to resolve itself into two warring camps, the champions of Clarissa and the defenders of Lovelace. But it is on this issue, in terms of the kind of power they wish to wield and the kind of fame they appear to seek, that the two characters reveal themselves as deeply akin. Clarissa's rebellion, too, centers on the kind of power she wishes to exercise over her virginity.

What Clarissa wants, she says, is "the single life." This option "was my choice," she announces, before she meets either Solmes or Lovelace (1: 123). But is it a real option? Early in the novel, it is easy enough to see in this wish merely fears of the prospect of marriage. This is the emotional trap women found themselves caught in—to guard fiercely and fear losing what in fact they were expected to give up. But such a double bind only reminds us that virginity in this culture was a means to an end and not an end in itself. Virginity as a vocation is a Catholic conception entirely foreign to a nation as fiercely Protestant as eighteenth-century England. Brides were to be virgins, yes, but virgins were eventually to be brides. The yielding of virginity at the proper time is, as we have seen, at least as much a social as a personal act, and the idea of a "single life" for a woman whose virginity has as much value as Clarissa's is profoundly threatening to the social order. For Clarissa to keep her virginity means, as her brother knows, that she will not "have to be what we would have her be." The kind of independence a virgin life implies is simply not acceptable, and this is the hard lesson Clarissa must learn. Before her illumination she seems, naively, to believe that her virginity is a token of her right to self-determination; what she learns instead is that it is the sign of her marketability. Lovelace knows the truth: "She never was in a state of *independency;* nor is it fit a woman should, of any age, or in any state of life" (3: 24).

This, then, is the context within which we must examine Clarissa's struggle to achieve her beloved single life. That struggle is finally not an expression of modesty in any way that her age approved, nor is it the result of what many of Clarissa's detractors, especially when the novel first appeared, have called her excessive reserve. Clarissa has assigned her maidenhead a kind of metaphysical significance, one that is deeply opposed to the kind of mercenary value it would normally have. For Clarissa, virginity metonymically suggests selfhood, and when it is lost, her pathetic cry is "I am no longer what I was in any one thing" (3: 205).

But who *is* Clarissa Harlowe, the "young lady" whose history we read at such great length? We know a good deal about what others would have her be—a dutiful daughter, a humiliated sister, an angel, a "woman in fact." We see her confusion about who she is, and Dr. Johnson's judgment is characteristically shrewd when he comments that "there is always something which she prefers to truth."[17] We learn what her activities and excellencies were before her long childhood idyll was interrupted by her coming of marriageable age: she managed the household, performed charitable works, and talked with both erudition and charm. She was, in short, the cynosure of the neighborhood, one whose reputation for beauty and virtue reached the trembling ears of Lovelace. When Clarissa, unconsciously but still unwillingly penetrated, cries, "I am no longer what I was," her lost maidenhead signifies the loss of all this—family, activity, and most profoundly, reputation. The girl who was the talk of the county has lost her virginity in the most anonymous way possible: in a secret house in a faceless city where no one knows her but the man who drugs and rapes her.

For Clarissa, in the immediate aftermath of the rape there is no connection between what she was and what she has become. She comes to learn, however, that her sometime fame and then apparent demise are both part of one trajectory. For a modern audience, it is easy to see that movement in feminist terms. Her identity as a paragon, Clarissa discovers, was not really a sign of her worth as an individual, an independent value that might logically culminate in "the single life," but rather a sign of her availability. As her mother tells her when the long Solmes nightmare begins, "If you mean to show your duty and your obedience, Clary, you must show it in *our* way; not in *your own*" (1: 78). In this light, Clarissa's rape is only a more open expression of the essential powerlessness of women in this culture. As Lovelace puts it, Clarissa never was "in a state of independency," for her virtue, her virgin state, is really a category created by this culture, a society in which she can have no solitary place.[18]

But just as Lovelace is more complicated than his occasional role as confused and questioning spokesman for his age would suggest, so Clarissa is a stronger figure than an understanding of her as patriarchal victim would allow. We saw in Lovelace a peculiar dualism, and he revealed himself as a character who feared the flesh and hoped for a spark of mind or spirit independent of any carnal taint. Clarissa, too, is or comes to be a dualist; she must reject her body, reject the life of the body in every sense, in order to be herself. Belford may have said that she seemed to him to be "all mind," but what Clarissa learns is that to the world she is not "mind" at all but a female body the world controls, and that to escape those snares she must escape her own imprisoning flesh. Finally, she rejects her body for two reasons: because she comes to believe that the sexuality of the body implies its literal corruptibility, its death, and because she discovers that, as a form of expression, the body is an unreliable text, always vulnerable to the demands of others.

The connection between sexuality and death surfaces early in the novel in Clarissa's repeated connection between marriage to the odious Solmes and premature burial (see 1: 87, 380), and the specifically sexual character of the metaphor emerges in a dream she has shortly before her elopement: "Methought my brother, my Uncle Antony, and Mr. Solmes, had formed a plot to destroy Mr. Lovelace; who discovering it, and believing I had a hand in it, turned all his rage against me. I thought he made them all fly into foreign parts upon it; and afterwards seizing upon me, carried me into a churchyard; and there, notwithstanding all my prayers and tears, and protestations of innocence, stabbed me to the heart, and then tumbled me into a deep grave ready dug, among two or three half-dissolved carcasses" (1:433). The dream transforms the image of premature burial into narrative. A man—Lovelace now, not Solmes as in the earlier premature-burial remarks, acknowledging that the rake is the real sexual threat—is explicitly the agent of death (still a living death: she is aware of her own burial), the death he deals out is clearly sexual, and the fruit of that sexual death is both degradation and putrefaction. For Clarissa, the phallus that will try her virginity is quite literally a worm. Penetration initiates corruption, and dissolution is the meaning of sexuality.

We see this idea elaborated both in Clarissa's own death and in Belford's description of the death of Mrs. Sinclair. Both reaffirm the connection of sex and death but do so in very different ways. Sinclair, the matriarch of sex in the novel, dies entirely appropriately of gangrene. As Belford paints the scene, the actual cause of the mortification, a broken leg, is completely submerged beneath the picture of sexualized flesh as decayed flesh. It is clear that the old dragon has been rotting a long time:

Her misfortune had not at all sunk, but rather, as I thought, increased her flesh; rage and violence perhaps swelling her muscular features. Behold her, then, spreading the whole tumbled bed with her huge, quaggy carcass: her mill-post arms held up; her broad hands clenched with violence; her big eyes, goggling and flaming red . . . ; her matted grizzly hair . . . spread about her fat ears and brawny neck; . . . her wide mouth, by reason of the contraction of her forehead . . . splitting her face, as it were, into two parts; and her huge tongue rolling hideously in it; heaving, puffing, as if for breath; her bellows-shaped and variously-colored breasts ascending by turns to her chin, and descending out of sight, with the violence of her gaspings. (4: 382)

Sinclair manages to combine both putrefaction and an increase in flesh, as though corruption were the natural element of such a body; her whorish flesh, Belford seems to say, thrives on dying.

The cause of Clarissa's death is a vexed question, because the novel offers no explicit diagnoses. She herself says it is "grief" (4: 305), and readers have filled in the gap by offering explanations ranging from consumption to anorexia.[19] The accusation of suicide has been leveled, and it is hard not to see something self-destructive in Clarissa's behavior, despite her claims to have avoided "all wilful neglects" (4: 13). But suicide is less a cause than an effect, and when we look for a cause, we cannot escape the way the novel enforces on us the connection between her rape and her sudden decline. That event alone marks the fulcrum between blooming good health and rapid decay. By his clinical vagueness here, Richardson compels us to look away from Clarissa's death as an organic process and see it symbolically. In that light, the cause of her death is as clear as it was in her nightmare: sexual penetration initiates bodily decay. The point is not, as some have suggested, that in the moral universe of this novel, a woman who has been dishonored, no matter how, must die; rather, Clarissa discovers that for her, sexuality *is* mortality.

We can see this thinking at work in the papers Clarissa scribbles in her delirium immediately after the rape. Paper 7 is typical:

Thou pernicious caterpillar, that preyest upon the fair leaf of virgin fame, and poisonest those leaves which thou canst not devour!

Thou fell blight, thou eastern blast, thou overspreading mildew, that destroyest the early promises of the shining year! that mockest the laborious toil, and blastest the joyful hopes of the painful husbandman!

Thou fretting moth, that corruptest the fairest garment!

Thou eating canker-worm, that preyest upon the opening bud, and turnest the damask rose into livid yellowness! (3: 207)

In her grief, Clarissa constructs powerful allegorical images of her demise. The experience of sexual intercourse has filled her head with every possible synonym for *rot: prey, poison, devour, mildew, blast, fret, corrupt, destroy, eat,* and so on. As in her dream, sexualized flesh—which is how she now regards her body—is not merely mortal; it is already and quite literally corrupted. The rake's creed may have erred in a fundamental way in Clarissa's case when it predicted, "Once subdued, always subdued," but in another sense, it was prophetic. Once she has been made flesh, treated as a "mere body," she is, she feels, doomed to *be* flesh—rotting flesh at that—as long as she lives.

But Clarissa is not Mrs. Sinclair: the old dragon is synonymous with the carnal freight that is her body, whereas Clarissa is able to discover that the body of death in which she is housed is not *her.* To be no longer what she was in any one thing turns out to be a liberation, one that enables her to reject what she calls "the encumbrance of body" (3: 321), slipping out of it as neatly as a snake shedding dead skin. A month after the rape, with her exit already well under way, she insists: "Let me repeat that I am quite sick of life; and of an earth in which *innocent* and *benevolent* spirits are sure to be considered as *aliens,* and to be made sufferers by the *genuine sons and daughters of that earth*" (3: 383).

Richardson's attitude toward sexuality has often been labeled "Puritan,"[20] but this kind of sentiment—and Clarissa's rejection of this world and its inevitable sexuality in general—has little to do with typical Puritan attitudes, which preached involvement in the world and promoted happy marriage. Milton's celebration of the nuptial bower was not a doctrinal aberration. Clarissa's sense of herself as an "alien spirit" and her belief that her investiture in an encumbering body is a kind of exile look back in some ways to older Roman Catholic doctrines of *contemptus mundi*. They are, at any rate, quite odd in eighteenth-century England and almost unheard of in the history of the English novel.

But they are not odd in this novel, where they bear at least some resemblance to Lovelace's own assumptions. Lovelace is not, let me hasten to add, an innocent or benevolent spirit, but he and Clarissa do share a suspicion of the body and its sexuality. He wishes to dominate it by the road of excess and destruction, and she by an ascetic path, but both are determined to achieve control. And that control does not suggest some classical ideal of harmony and moderation, and certainly it does not suggest Christian humility; what they both want is triumph. As we have seen, Lovelace largely rejects the social world he inhabits, and seeks its overthrow; Clarissa, the "alien spirit," seeks simply to escape. The only single life is, she learns, in another world, and she begins to prepare for her journey there as soon as she feels she knows what the genuine sons and daughters of this earth really want. Finally, both characters are alien spirits, and both exhibit a memorable contempt for the mundane ties that society lives by.

There is another, related reason that Clarissa rejects her body and departs this world, and that is her discovery that her body is an unreliable text, incapable of expressing the self she wishes to make legible. Lovelace wants to read her body, she wants it to speak reliably who she is, and both are frustrated. Look again at one comment she makes after the rape: "Thou pernicious caterpillar, that preyest upon the fair leaf of virgin fame, and poisonest those leaves which thou canst not devour!" The important words are *fair leaf of virgin fame*, a phrase so richly suggestive of the action of the whole novel that it is worth pausing over. First, the words suggest what Clarissa's reputation was. Before Lovelace, she was a "famous" virgin, a young woman whose reputation for modesty and virtue was widespread. But her fame was also "virginal": as Lovelace puts it, echoing her parents, "What have been her trials?" That is, her fame is untested. Moreover, the "fair leaf" suggests the beauty of the text she believes her fame makes visible, but it paradoxically implies a virginal whiteness—a tabula rasa, a blank page. There is a problem here: how can a page be both blank and full of repute? Can emptiness be famous? For Clarissa, it appears that her maidenhead is a page, a text that signifies only by being intact and unmarked, a dangerously vulnerable position, since its blankness invites others to mark it. And that is exactly what "caterpillars" like Lovelace or her family want to do. In controlling her virginity, they make her fame their own and create a self for her that is to their own liking: "Now must she be what we would have her be."

One central crisis for Clarissa is her confrontation with the power of signification of her own body, and the struggles we have looked at in such detail are battles to control what her body says. But the "fair leaf," like the single life, is not really possible in this world. Still, there is a solution, Clarissa decides. If the body cannot be a substitute for words, then perhaps words can replace the body. Instead of the text of the body—penetrable, corruptible, or simply inscrutable—she will construct another kind of body, one of words. After the illumination that the rape affords her, her task becomes the creation of this new body, one she believes will be unambiguous and untouchable. Fame cannot be an absence or an emptiness, and she will fill the vessel of her life, make her name, by the new text that she creates. The fair leaf will be darkened, but the marks will be her own or ones she believes she controls. If a body cannot speak the truth, perhaps a book can.[21]

The struggle among the Harlowes, Lovelace, and Clarissa for the control of her virginity is thus about much more than a maidenhead, and it is part of Richardson's genius that he can make this issue so resonant. If we can abstract one thread from this complexity, however, we might say that all the main players in this drama are engaged in the process of building a name, a labor in which Clarissa's virginity is an indispensable commodity. The Harlowes want a peerage, a social elevation of their name. Their control of Clarissa is crucial: if she becomes what they would have her be, then they will become what they themselves desire. Lovelace wants a name in rakish annals, the immortality he will gain by the conquest of the paragon Harlowe. Even Clarissa, who had wanted virgin fame and who chooses to leave a world she despises, becomes her book, sublimating her unstable flesh into what she thinks will be the shield of language. After all, the book we read bears her name. *Name* is perhaps the most common metonymy for fame or reputation, and the heroic quest all these characters engage in is the attempt to gain that self-transcending yet still somehow personal immortality that heroes achieve. Deeds, in the end, must become words in order to survive, and the name lives on as the shorthand repository for all that a hero has done. Lovelace seems correct when he bemoans his heroic belatedness and rails at a fate that sends him after virgins rather than kingdoms. As we saw in Defoe, the quest for a heroic name in the novel as a genre will always play itself out in a smaller and more limited world than that in which the epic hero could enact his desire. But Lovelace's frustration is only more self-conscious than Clarissa's. Here, too, these characters are akin, and both are versions of Eliot's mixed hero, with "a certain . . . grandeur ill-matched with the meanness of opportunity." What we see is that the ancient need to make a name and thus defeat mortality persists, and Richardson has almost miraculously elevated what could have been (and in *Pamela*, largely was) a petty squabble over what Blake called "a little curtain of flesh" into an infinitely rich exploration of humanity's oldest story, the struggle to make a name that will not die.

I promised at the outset of this discussion to conclude by stepping back from the consideration of character and looking at *Clarissa* in relation to Richardson and his audience. That is not a straightforward task. Take Lovelace, for example. Richardson said of his male lead, "I *intend* [Lovelace] to be unamiable," and he confessed, after publication, that "I thought I had made him too wicked, too Intriguing, too revengeful, . . . for him to obtain the Favour and good Wishes of any worthy Heart of *either* Sex." The confusion he betrays in the last remark was provoked by letters from readers like Lady Bradshaigh, who insisted that "if I was to die for it, I cannot help being fond of Lovelace. A sad dog! why would you make him so wicked and yet so agreeable?"[22] Both authorial intention and reader response here seem to be only superficially related to the character we have examined. On the one side, Richardson appears to want to ignore the splendid complexity and contradiction of Lovelace and make him a mere prop in a homily. On the other, Lady Bradshaigh at least recognizes Lovelace's complexity, but the frisson of mingled fear and desire that he provokes in her is a cliché—proper lady meets dashing rake and falls into a confused flutter. Her reaction probably helped confirm Richardson's judgment that the doctrine of the reformed rake was "too commonly received," but neither she nor Richardson tells us much that is useful about where the Lovelace of the novel comes from or what his appearance in midcentury England says about that world.

John Traugott insists that we make a distinction between the Richardson of public pronouncements and the Richardson who wrote *Clarissa*[23]—not always an easy task, given the way the former has left his fingerprints all over the work of the latter. But I think that all readers of the novel would do well to keep the distinction in mind. The first Richardson has always tended to be a figure of fun, but the desperate spectacle of his attempts to translate the meaning of his masterpiece into banal doctrines is more pathetic than humorous—pathetic and irrelevant, for there is nothing banal about *Clarissa*, which Harold Bloom recently called the "finest novel in the English language."[24] Intelligent readers may disagree about that precise ranking, but there is no denying that Richardson's achievement here is startling, both as a deeply subversive commentary on the age and especially as the creation of a world of character such as literature had perhaps never before seen. Let me consider each of these points briefly in conclusion.

The endlessly fascinating people that Richardson created, whatever he may have claimed to be doing, represent profoundly subversive tendencies—against marital exchange, against the double standard, against even the social order itself. It is especially difficult to connect the Richardson who imagined all this with the one who, for instance, claimed that the moral of his long tale was "that in all reciprocal Duties the non-Performance of the Duty on one Part is not an Excuse for the Failure of the Other."[25] Indeed, and the lesson of *King Lear* is, Don't ask your children too many questions. In particular, Lovelace and Clarissa suggest that the world of sexuality and all that flows from it—courtship, marriage, the family, the very construction of gender—are corrupt and irredeemable, a nightmare on all sides. This is a very odd stance for an English novel to take, for novels in general, even when they are tragic (as in *Wuthering Heights*), normally celebrate the possibilities of love and most often affirm the institution of marriage as the cornerstone of social order. Perhaps we have here the central reason that all those early readers wanted Richardson to change his mind and give them, at the end of the novel, a happily married Lovelace and Clarissa. Such a conclusion would detoxify what was—and is—a very scary book.

A century later, a writer like Dickens had no recourse; he submitted to public pressure, and Pip and Estella were most improbably joined.

With Defoe, we found that it was more useful to analyze the psychology of heroism than the inner working of the individual character. With Richardson, however, we enter a different world, a specifically interior world that is both rich and strange. In devoting the bulk of this chapter to a discussion of the Harlowes, Lovelace, and Clarissa, I find myself in the primary tradition of Richardson criticism, which has (even in its most modern permutations)[26] never strayed far from issues of character: motivations, mistakes, discoveries, and the like. At the risk of sounding intolerably banal myself, I would venture to say that this discussion forms the main line of commentary on Richardson's fiction simply because we *can* do it. This kind of interpretation is so deeply satisfying and enjoyable that I am almost tempted to say that the novel appeared on the narrative scene so that readers would have these kinds of characters to analyze. It is astonishing to remember that they are only words on a page.

3

Tom Jones:
The Treachery of Language

Richardson, it is clear, believed in the power of language, but perhaps he believed too naively. If his struggles to control audience response tell us anything, they speak of his conviction—his rather desperate conviction—that words can be transparent, that an author can finally make language speak what he wants it to, and that words bent to his desire will, in turn, enforce the assent of his readers. It is equally clear that Henry Fielding harbored no such illusions, and the experience of reading *Tom Jones* constitutes (among many other things) an extended confrontation with the slipperiness of all language. Let me hasten to add that Fielding's skepticism about language does not make him any prophet of poststructuralism—he does believe that something we can identify as "the truth" exists. But like his comic and satiric predecessor Swift, Fielding is suspicious of most expressions of the truth, especially those which claim that truth ever appears to us in any self-evident form. As a result of this suspicion, Fielding is typically less concerned to promote any particular doctrine as "true" than he is to develop an attitude toward all doctrine, and he works to achieve that end by insisting that we recognize both the variety and the potential treachery of human expression.

Let me clarify at the outset more precisely what I mean both by *language* and by *truth*. As I will use *language,* I mean by it any form of meaningful expression. In this broad sense, anything that communicates meaning (even false or misleading meanings) is a language, and so my use of *language* will include not only speech and writing but physical gestures, clothing, appearances, and so on. The definition of *truth*, of course, ranges from a simple "that which is verifiable" to the ultimate questions of the meaning of existence. My aims here with regard to the truth are modest, as I believe Fielding's were. When I say that he believes in truth, I mean that he believes—with nearly all his contemporaries—in the reality of right and wrong: Tom is right to save Mrs. Waters from Northerton, wrong to become Lady Bellaston's kept man. In this chapter, I will spend little time on the question of Fielding's particular beliefs about right and wrong and will pay much closer attention to the more specific question of what truths various kinds of language are able—or unable—to communicate.[1] How does one say, "I am in love"; how does one say, "I am worthy"?

Any discussion of language in *Tom Jones* must first of all acknowledge the remarkable variety of kinds of *speech*. In contrast to an early fiction like *Jonathan Wild*, in which Fielding gives us little direct conversation and most of the dialogue is delivered as indirect discourse, in *Tom Jones* we are confronted with a multitude of sharply distinguished voices. The most powerful voice of all, it goes almost without saying, belongs to the narrator himself. He is, in the minds of many, the most important "character" in the book,[2] one who amuses and instructs, withholds and reveals, praises and blames, but is always, it seems, himself a stable, even godlike figure, building the great architecture of the novel, with his clear signature on every block of stone. But this is a novel of voices, voices that often seem as narrow as they are distinct. We can think of Western's radically limited vocabulary, a rudimentary dialect that at times seems to consist only of "shat ha un, d——m me, shat ha un" (802). There is the speech of Partridge, a schoolmaster whose Latin is not only bad but confined to a few tags that he repeats again and again—an instance of a whole language and literature reduced to a collection of clichés. And these two are no more narrow than Thwackum and Square, with their endless reiterations of the "divine Power of Grace" and the "natural Beauty of Virtue" (126). In fact, everyone's speech seems in some way limited, and the novel is filled with the special talk of servants, soldiers, innkeepers, shrews, cuckolds, lawyers, doctors, gypsies, the clergy, and courtesans. Some characters, like the Man of the Hill or Mrs. Fitzpatrick, spend many pages telling us their stories, and Fielding is at great pains to show that these apparently ingenuous narrators are powerfully self-serving; that is, they can only talk about themselves. Di Western talks politics, Allworthy makes moral pronouncements, Mrs. Honour speaks of her "position." Such limitations on the speech of characters seem to be part of Fielding's indebtedness to the tradition of the comedy of humors, but I believe that he is up to something more than the successful employment of an ancient and effective comic technique. Such limitations in what people can and do say begin to suggest the problems Fielding sees in language in general. As an interpreter of the expressions of others, how does anyone arrive at the truth behind what they are saying?

Something of the way Fielding wants us to think about language and expression comes through at two crucial moments in the novel, one near the beginning, the other very close to the end.[3] In the first, we find Allworthy and Mrs. Wilkins discussing what to do with the infant that the Squire has just discovered in his bed. Mrs. Wilkins says:

> "If I might be so bold to give my Advice, I would have it put in a Basket, and sent out and laid at the Church-Warden's Door. It is a good Night, only a little rainy and windy; and if it was well wrapt up, and put in a warm Basket, it is two to one but it lives till it is found in the Morning. . . ."
> There were some Strokes in this Speech, which, perhaps, would have offended Mr. *Allworthy*, had he strictly attended to it; but he had now got one of his Fingers into the Infant's Hand, which by its gentle Pressure, seeming to implore his Assistance, had certainly out-pleaded the Eloquence of Mrs. *Deborah*. (41)

What we see juxtaposed here are the cruel words of Mrs. Wilkins and the mute eloquence of the infant foundling. Put another way, we hear two different kinds of language, one verbal, one physical, both competing for Allworthy's attention and judgment. Crucially, given that susceptibility to the power of speech that we will see elsewhere, the Squire does not really *hear* Mrs. Wilkins and, perhaps as a result, makes what we know is the right choice here—to keep Tom.

In a parallel scene in London, Allworthy confronts Bilfil about his dealings with Lawyer Dowling, while his landlady, Mrs. Miller, looks on. Allworthy asks his nephew

> "whether he knew any Thing of Mr. *Dowling's* having seen any of the Persons who were present at the Duel between *Jones* and another Gentleman?"
> There is nothing so dangerous as a Question which comes by Surprize on a Man whose Business it is to conceal Truth, or to defend Falsehood. For which Reason, those worthy Personages, whose noble Office it is to save the Lives of their Fellow-Creatures at the *Old-Bailey*, take the utmost Care . . . to divine every Question which may be asked their Clients on

the Day of Trial, that they may be supply'd with proper and ready Answers. . . . Besides, the sudden and violent Impulse on the Blood, occa-
sioned by these Surprizes, causes frequently such an Alteration in the
Countenance, that the Man is obliged to give Evidence against himself.
And such indeed were the Alterations which the Countenance of *Blifil*
underwent from this sudden Question, that we can scarce blame the Eager-
ness of Mrs. *Miller,* who immediately cry'd out, "Guilty, upon my Honour!
Guilty, upon my Soul!" (932)

Mrs. Miller, like Mrs. Wilkins, is suspicious but rightfully so,
while Blifil, unlike the infant Tom, relies on speech to plead his
case. The result, however, is the same: male "eloquence" triumphs
over female suspicion, and Blifil is able to extricate himself by a
typically clever speech, one that combines self-concealment and
self-justification, explaining that he sent Dowling to suborn the
witnesses in Tom's favor, rather than the opposite. Here again, we
see the body in competition with speech as modes of expression
and as vehicles of truth. In the later scene, that conflict takes place
not between rival "speakers" like the unknown infant and Mrs.
Wilkins but internally—Blifil, as it were, speaks in two ways and so
contradicts himself. Unfortunately in this instance, Allworthy lis-
tens to the unreliable but powerful evidence of Blifil's words rather
than, as earlier, to the mute but eloquent evidence of the body.
Words here speak louder, if less truthfully, than actions. It is a part
of Allworthy's failure throughout the novel that he typically gives
speech priority as the bearer of truth. For instance, the "trials" of
both Partridge and Tom miscarry because they speak poorly in
defense of themselves against linguistically more powerful adver-
saries. The effect of these two scenes is to remind the reader that
we are faced with a variety of languages—some true, some not—
and that our difficult task is to sort out which expressions are false.

In this novel of errors, the mistake that is perhaps the most
important provides us with an excellent example of the way the
signifying power of the body can be ignored. I refer to the assumption that Jenny Jones is Tom's mother. When that eager detective
Mrs. Wilkins sets out to discover what local woman bore the orphan, she decides that Jenny is "the likeliest Person to have committed this Fact" (48). And was she so likely because, in this small
community, everyone noticed the unmistakable significance of a
swollen belly (as all will later notice the visible sign of Molly's

condition)? No, assusation lights upon Jenny because of her knowledge of Latin and "a new Silk Gown" (49), acquisitions deemed
unnatural and unfit for a person of her serving status. Jenny, of
course, admits her "crime" (a stand-in role for which the silk gown
was probably advance payment from Bridget), but she can successfully carry off the deception only because no one brings up the
question of whether she ever actually appeared to be pregnant.
Jenny's pregnancy is, in a sense, hysterical—but not because it
existed in *her* mind. It existed only in the minds of her accusers,
who, for evidence of the truth, look not to her body but to what
they believe is the unmistakable significance of her Latin and her
gown. Those pieces of evidence are, for these observers, as indica-
tive as if Jenny wore a scarlet *A*—they "speak" of sexual crime. In
other words, a rigid class code that dictates the education and dress
appropriate for all levels of society is one "language" in which this
community firmly believes, and that belief carries with it an assumption of some kind of guilt whenever the code is violated.
Jenny and Bridget are able to make their deception work because
they appear to know that these assumptions are so strong that no
one will bother to ask the staggeringly obvious question, Did Jenny
look pregnant? With both Blifil and Jenny, then, the body can speak
the truth and be ignored because it is less privileged than other
forms of expression.

It is important to qualify the point here. I am not trying to establish some equivalence between Henry Fielding and, say, D. H.
Lawrence. Fielding does not juxtapose the language of speech and
that of the body in order to valorize the latter in some kind of
absolute way. For one thing, as we will see, the body can lie too.
The point instead is that, throughout *Tom Jones*, Fielding sets up
rival modes of expression to show that truth may express itself in
various forms and that we are obliged to recognize how fallible our
understanding of "language" really is. When presented with any
kind of expression, we tend, it seems, to make mistakes—to over-
look, to mishear, to misinterpret. The doctrine here is not about the
truth of the body or the truth of any other form of language; it is
about humility, especially humility regarding our ability to see the
truth. Having made that point, I will now proceed to a more detailed examination of three issues: sexuality, class and/or birth, and
hypocrisy. Each of these issues represents a kind of language (or
produces its own distinctive language), and together they provide

a sense of the range of Fielding's thinking about the problems and possibilities of human expression.

First, sexuality. In the middle of Tom's liaison with Lady Bellaston, Fielding describes one of her visits to Tom's lodgings this way: "It would be tedious to give the particular Conversation which consisted of very common and ordinary Occurrences, and which lasted from two till six o'clock in the Morning" (717). The "Conversation" that is passed over is, of course, sexual, and Fielding's implication here (and elsewhere—compare 693, 699, and 722) is that sex is a kind of invariant expression, "common and ordinary" and so well known to his audience that particulars would be boring. The passage provokes several responses. We smile at the narrator's ironic combination of the decorous and the titillating— we recognize that by leading our attention away from these "Occurrences," he thereby heightens our interest in them. But Fielding is also making a more serious point here. His dismissive refusal to talk about sex has the effect of reminding us that sex is one form of human activity that most of us talk about a great deal, one that we discuss, moreover, in very particular ways. Sex, too, has a language, but it is one in which there tends to be a comic discrepancy between the extravagance of its signifiers and what for Fielding is the very "common and ordinary" thing they are signifying.

Fielding's portrayal of courtship in the novel provides a good illustration of what he is trying to say about the language of sex. Courtship is not, of course, an exclusively sexual activity, but it does typically carry sexual implications. Yet the sexuality of courtship, especially in a proper society like middle- and upper-class England in the eighteenth century, is largely displaced onto language, in the sense of both speech and gesture. With this notion in mind, let us look at Blifil's first visit to Sophia as a suitor, "a Picture of formal Courtship in Miniature" (293), remembering all the while that he has designs upon not only her fortune but also her "person":

Mr. *Blifil* soon arrived; and Mr. *Western* soon after withdrawing, left the young Couple together.

Here a long Silence of near a Quarter of an Hour ensued: For the Gentleman who was to begin the Conversation had all the unbecoming Modesty which consists in Bashfulness. He often attempted to speak, and as often suppressed his Words just at the very Point of Utterance. At last out they broke in a Torrent of far-fetched and high-strained Compliments, which were answered, on her Side, by downcast Looks, half Bows and civil Monosyllables. (294)

We are struck first, perhaps, by Blifil's silence in the scene; he is, after all, the character in the novel for whom, more than anyone else, plausible speech seems always at the ready. But we have to remember that silence is part of the language of courtship—a tongue-tied lover, if we know the conventions, is still expressing himself. We have by this point in the novel developed a healthy dislike for Blifil, and so we laugh here at what seems to be his egregious conventionality, at his inability to be spontaneous. In this scene, what we observe is indeed "formal Courtship"—courtship in form only, by the book. Our laughter, however, is both more complicated and darker than a simple response to the picture of a rule-bound suitor, for what is also funny here is that Blifil's formal behavior seems so thoroughly opposed to his real and villainous sexual desire for Sophia—he wants, we learn later, to "rifle her charms" (346). In other words, we have a mode of expression, "formal Courtship," that serves as a screen for the sadistic sexuality behind it. Sex has been turned into a hopelessly deceptive language.

It is easy enough to mark this episode down as yet another instance of Blifil's hypocrisy, another place where he is able to hide base motives behind correct social forms.[4] But Fielding refuses to allow us to rest easy with that complacent judgment, for he immediately follows this scene with a conversation between Tom and Sophia that bears a striking—and disturbing—similarity to its predecessor:

He presently ran to her, and with a Voice full at once of Tenderness and Terrour, cried, "O my *Sophia*, what means this dreadful Sight!"—She looked softly at him for a Moment before she spoke, and then said, "Mr. *Jones*, for Heaven's Sake, how came you here?—Leave me, I beseech you, this Moment." "Do not," says he, "impose so harsh a Command upon me—my Heart bleeds faster than those Lips. O *Sophia*, how easily could I drain my Veins to preserve one Drop of that dear Blood." . . . A few Moments now passed in Silence between these Lovers, while his Eyes were eagerly fixed on *Sophia*, and hers declining towards the Ground. (298)

What are Tom's words here but a "Torrent of far-fetched and high-strained Compliments?" And is it a sufficient defense to say of

them that we "know" they are sincere, while Blifil's are hypocritical? I think not. Fielding is underlining, by this comic juxtaposition
of similar language in the mouths of morally opposing characters,
the fact that we all sound foolish and conventional when we talk
about love or sex, for the simple reason that where this activity is
concerned, we all have the same language to use. The comedy
consists in the discrepancy between a "far-fetched" lanugage and
the "ordinary Occurrences" we want it to describe. But there is also
a serious point embedded here: if both hero and villain, both lover
and sadist, sound alike, how do we tell them apart?

Any hasty tendency on our part to validate the language of the
body as somehow truer than other forms of speech is undercut:
Fielding is acutely aware of the way we constantly turn the life of the
body into words, and words are a very treacherous commodity—as
is, for that matter, the body itself. The problems posed by sexuality
and speech dominate one of the most famous—and funniest—
scenes in the novel, Tom's encounter in the woods with Molly.
Briefly, a drunken Tom wanders about the forest, bemoaning in the
most elevated language both the depth and impossibility of his love
for Sophia. Just as he takes out his knife to carve her initials on a tree,
he meets Molly; after a brief "Parley," they retire "into the thickest
Part of the Grove" (257). Throughout the chapter, Tom and the narrator seem to compete to see whose language will prove the most "far-
fetched." Tom, for instance, insists,

> O *Sophia*, would Heaven give thee to my Arms, how blest would be my
> Condition! Curst be that Fortune which sets a Distance between us. Was I
> but possessed of thee, one only Suit of Rags thy whole Estate, is there a
> Man on Earth whom I would envy! How contemptible would the brightest
> *Circassian* Beauty . . . appear to my eyes! But why do I mention another
> Woman? . . . No, my *Sophia*, if cruel Fortune separates us for ever, my Soul
> shall doat on thee alone. The chastest Constancy will I ever preserve to thy
> Image. . . . Oh! my fond Heart is so wrapt in that tender Bosom, that the
> brightest Beauties would have for me no Charms, nor would a Hermit be
> colder in their Embraces. (256)

But such ludicrous speech is embedded in equally ludicrous narra-
tion: "It was now a pleasant Evening in the latter End of *June*, when
our Heroe was walking in a most delicious Grove, where the gentle
Breezes fanning the Leaves, together with the sweet Trilling of a

murmuring Stream, and the melodious Notes of Nightingales
formed all together the most enchanting Harmony. . . . While . . .
his lively Imagination painted the charming Maid in various ravish-
ing Forms, his warm Heart melted with Tenderness, and at length
throwing himself on the Ground by the Side of a gently murmuring
Brook, he broke forth into the following Ejaculation" (255–56).
Here is prose worthy of the imagination of Gertie Macdowell. Even
this tough-minded and worldly narrator, it seems, falls prey to
cliché when the subject is love. He goes on, however, to let us
know that *he*, at least, understands the foolishness of such language by the simple expedient of continuing to use it even though
its subject has changed from Sophia to Molly—which is to say, from
"love" to "sex": "[Tom] beheld—not his *Sophia*—no, nor a *Circassian*
Maid richly and elegantly attired for the Grnd Signoir's Seraglio.
No; without a Gown, in a Shift that was somewhat of the coarsest,
and none of the cleanest, bedewed likewise with some odiferous
Effluvia, the Produce of the Day's Labour, with a Pitch-fork in her
Hand, *Molly Seagrim* approached" (256). As the object of description moves down the social scale, the language, which remains the
same,[5] is automatically transformed in significance and becomes
mock-heroic. But the ridiculousness of such speech, when applied
to Molly, enforces a more general skepticism. Suddenly, the whole
chapter—Tom and Sophia, as well as Tom and Molly—seems
mock-heroic, and the language of "love" again comes across as an
attempt to dress up the common and ordinary in language that is
irretrievably high strained. The narrator emphasizes this shift by
falling silent at the moment when what we might call "meaningful
expression" begins: "Here ensued a Parley, which, as I do not think
myself obliged to relate it, I shall omit" (257).

The contrast that Fielding draws here works on several levels. We
see the way in which a certain kind of speech becomes a form of self-
delusion. Tom's use of conventional language becomes a way to lie
to himself about the strength of his fidelity. The whole scene, in fact,
is a series of lies, both verbal and physical—perhaps Fielding's way
of commenting on the old maxim *in vino veritas*. He emphasizes
Tom's drunkenness, but the drunken man apparently expresses himself no more accurately than a sober one. Neither Tom's bibulous
peroration on Sophia nor his parley with Molly—that is, neither his
words of love nor his sexual actions—are adequate expressions of
the truth about his feelings. He is not as faithful as he says, and he is

not as wanton as he appears. His inability to express himself accurately may reflect his essential confusion; Fielding has just told us that "DRUNKENNESS SHEWS THE MIND OF A MAN, AS A MIRROUR REFLECTS HIS PERSON" (250). And lest we fall into the trap of thinking that the body speaks truer than words, in the next chapter we see Blifil, Thwackum, and Square putting their own mistaken and self-serving interpretation on Tom's silent "conversation" with Molly. They assume—quite wrongly—that they know what it means.

The chapter thus leaves us with a memorable and wonderfully comic sense of the discrepancy between those biological urges which are part of what we mean by *love* and the grotesquely inflated language in which we dress up those urges. The juxtaposition of competing modes of expression, here as elsewhere, finally has the effect of making us regard all language and all expression skeptically. After all, even our dominating narrator loses track of the business of his perfect plot for a minute here. He is apparently so enamored of the amatory language he employs that he places Tom's walk at "the latter end of June." As Battestin points out, this date is a chronological impossibility in terms of the time scheme of the novel, but I believe that the "mistake" is Fielding's deliberate reminder of just how silly and artificial the language of love is. In the self-deceiving mind of the lover, it is always the month of June.[6]

Several times already in this discussion the issue of class has come up (with respect to Jenny Jones and Molly Seagrim), and we need to think about class in *Tom Jones* as another kind of language that Fielding wishes to examine. The issue is particularly complex because Fielding is no leveler; class distinctions are both real and right for him. At the same time, however, the skepticism that we have seen elsewhere marks Fielding's thinking about this issue as well. Considerations of class pervade the novel, but I think we can usefully concentrate on the questions that surround the identity of the hero, Tom Jones.

Tom's appearance in Allworthy's bed at the beginning of the story is an action that demands an antecedent: where did he come from? Without knowledge of his origin, no one, it appears, can be confident who he is, a confusion that is confirmed by what we might call Tom's multiple parenting. He is biologically assigned to Jenny Jones and Partridge, thus making him the offspring of a criminal liaison in the lower classes and ensuring that he is "born to be hanged" (118). Biology is destiny, and the original crime will reproduce itself. Nevertheless, Tom is adopted by Allworthy, who gives him his own Christian name and raises him as a gentleman. In the popular mind, such gratuitous generosity is unnatural and makes sense only if Tom is Allworthy's illegitimate son. Such an unnatural affection, that is, is explicable if Tom is—in the language of the period—Allworthy's "natural" son. And he has other "fathers" as well—Black George, to whom Tom is so foolishly loyal, and especially Western, who informally adopts Tom as his hunting son. There is a way in which Tom enters into a filial relationship—real or imagined, formal or informal—with almost everyone in the neighborhood. The obvious result is profound confusion, for both Tom and those around him. He is both a gentleman and, in Blifil's phrase, a "beggarly Bastard" (130). The misconceptions that surround his identity finally all point to, if I may say it, his *missed* conception. Tom is a kind of free-floating signifier, one who can mean anything, a character whom no one can read or know with any certainty so long as where he comes from is unclear.

But that mysterious conception, that missing sexual act which generates both Tom and his story, also points to Tom's powerfully meaningful place in what amounts to a sterile world, for if he is, in class terms, a floating signifier with no clear ground of meaning, he is also, in another sense, specifically significant. Tom is a sign of the fertility that is missing from the neighborhood of Paradise Hall. The little world of Somerset where Tom is born is remarkably barren, so barren, in fact, that in addition to the other elements of romance that many have seen in the novel, we could add that Paradise Hall and environs amount to a kind of wasteland.[7] By the end of book 2, we have encountered two widowers (Allworthy and Western), several spinsters (Bridget, Mrs. Wilkins), and two bad marriages (the Blifils and the Partridges), both of which end with the death of one spouse. That is, entering *Tom Jones* we enter an unmarried world, in which there are only two children, the insufferable half-orphan Blifil (a misconception if ever there was one) and Tom, who appears on the scene by an act of apparently spontaneous generation. As such, Tom comes to represent a rogue principle of fertility, one who will remain roguish as long as he seems to represent reproduction outside a legitimate social structure. The fact that he is surrounded by incestuous possibility throughout the book—gossip links him to Bridget; as Western's hunting son, he is a kind of brother to Sophia; and of course he beds Jenny Jones/Waters—is Fielding's way of emphasizing how potentially dangerous Tom is, how dangerous sexuality is, outside of any social structure.

His problematic status is emphasized by his curious name, Jones. As one landlady he will meet on the road asks, "Why doth he not go by the Name of his Father?" (417). Lacan has sensitized us to the possibility that the "name of the father" is something like an ultimate signifier, the ground of all meaning and especially of all law.[8] Tom, however, odd fellow that he is, goes by the name of his mother, or the woman who claims to be his mother, even though his paternity has supposedly been determined. The effect of his matrilineal name is again to suggest the impossibility of placing Tom within any kind of structure, either familial or social. And class, in eighteenth-century England, is undeniably a dominant social structure, one designed to confer immediate meaning about everyone's identity. As such, it is meant to be another kind of language, but it is a language in which Tom seems to be unable to express any stable meaning. He can represent, on the one hand, the renewal of a decayed social order (one that is barren and largely without love) and, on the other, the threat of its extinction (through incest and other sexual crimes). At first sight of Tom, virtually everyone in the novel wants either to sleep with him or to adopt him (though his vulnerability to older women like Mrs. Waters or Lady Bellaston makes even this distinction difficult). Problems arise because he lacks any knowledge of his true origin: it turns out to be impossible for him to say who he is. In the terms of the language of class, Tom is quite mute. Names, too, are a language, but Tom's name tells us only what he cannot say—who he is. If the name of the father is the bedrock of all law, what Tom's name signifies is that he has no mark of the law upon him. No wonder we see him first as an interloper and then as a thief and that the common belief is that he is born to be hanged.

Once Tom is exiled from Paradise Hall and takes to the road, the confusion about his identity becomes more acute and reveals quite clearly the way in which Fielding's society depends on a knowledge of class. The question that Tom encounters again and again is whether he is what he appears to be. For example, we repeatedly hear how handsome he is. Lady Bellaston's evaluation, "He is a very pretty Fellow" (693), only echoes the judgment of everyone whom he meets. But Tom's good looks are not only a sexual signifier; they also appear to say something about his class. Seeing that handsome face, people read him as a gentleman. The Lieutenant, whose company of soldiers Tom almost joins, is struck "at . . . first Sight" by the fact that this young man is "naturally genteel" with "a remarkable Air of Dignity in his look" (370). As the doctor who treats Tom after Northerton's attack puts it, "I've a Gentleman under my Hands, have I not?" (412). Yet throughout the road section of the novel, Tom is consistently exposed—his illegitimate origin is discovered, his lack of money is revealed, and people's reaction to him almost invariably reverses from initial pleasure to condemnation. The very first innkeeper Tom meets sets the pattern. After first welcoming Tom, he later ends by saying, "I shall use no . . . Civility towards him: For it seems, for all his laced Waistcoat there, he is no more a Gentleman than myself; but a poor Parish Bastard . . . now turned out of Doors" (365).

The problem is that everyone wants class signifiers to be a reliable indication of personal worth. Often in the eighteenth-century novel, a character who projects a class appearance at odds with his or her true status is literally criminal. We think of Moll Flanders's disguises or Lovelace's dressing up the whores to play the part of his highborn relations. To give out misleading class signals is a form of fraud. On his journey to London, Tom is rather like a counterfeit coin, repeatedly accepted and then found to ring false. More precisely, Tom is a *potential* counterfeit—perhaps a beggarly bastard, perhaps something else. An unambiguous fraud presents a simpler case. But Tom cannot be placed, cannot be read with security. Sophia is exceptional when she says, "I know none with such Perfections. So brave, and yet so gentle; so witty, yet so inoffensive; so humane, so civil, so genteel, so handsome! What signifies his being base-born, when compared with such Qualifications as these?" (288). For her, Tom's meaning is stable, whatever his birth. In the language of class, however, birth is the privileged signifier, and the fact that Tom may be baseborn renders his wit, his gentility, and his good looks not merely irrelevant but positively dangerous. In the eyes of the world, that possible discrepancy between looks and birth is Tom's real crime, far more than his game-poaching, drunkenness, or wenching. This is a world that wants class signifiers to be true.

One way to think about this issue is to consider the difference between what we call identity and character. As I use the term, *identity* suggests those elements of a personality which are external: name, birth, class, occupation, education, style—everything, in short, that the world can see. *Character,* then, sums up those things which are internal: emotions, habits of mind, conscience, ideas, qualities like generosity or selfishness—everything, that is, that the world must infer on the basis of externalized signs. I think it is no exaggeration to say that the real struggle for Tom throughout the novel is to make his character and his identity coincide. Because his identity is unstable, because the language his appearance speaks seems to the world to be deceptive or contradictory, people lose faith in their instinctive sense that his character is that of a "naturally" good man. Now there are, of course, a number of people who do recognize and respond to the goodness of Tom's character; Sophia, Nightingale, Mrs. Miller, and others do not reverse their initial and instinctive approval. But Allworthy's disillusionment and Tom's exile from Paradise Hall describe a pattern that haunts Fielding's hero. It is as if the dissonance of inner and outer that people believe they discover in Tom marks him as that most dangerous of sinners, the hypocrite, for what is a hypocrite except one whose identity misleads us about his character?

From all these matters, it is hard to sort out Fielding's own thinking on the issue of class. Certainly it would be a gross misrepresentation to assert that he is mounting any kind of conscious attack on the class system of mid-eighteenth-century England. Tom is, of course, *not* "base-born," and his gentility is revealed in the end as the product of what can only be called good breeding, not that of a personal worth separable from the circumstances of his origin. We can contrast Tom's discoveries here with those of Pip—*Great Expectations* turns into a kind of inverted *Tom Jones* in which the gentleman discovers he really was baseborn. But it is equally impossible to suppose that Fielding is complacent about class issues. Even when we do not know who Tom is, we despise Blifil for his "beggarly Bastard" comment, and we cringe every time an innkeeper condemns him. Because we learn Tom's "true" identity only after long acquaintance with his character, we are left at the end of the novel with an explanation of that character that is in some way still incomplete. The missing origin has been filled in, the name of the father has been supplied, and the assurance of the narrator and the obvious comic form of the novel kept us reasonably secure all along. We are, however, left uncomfortably to contemplate the possibility that this comic discovery might never have been made, that Tom might have been left—quite literally—to hang in the limbo of nonidentity that has haunted him throughout. The distinction we must make is between class as value and class as language. What Fielding appears to want to do is to affirm the former and teach us, again, considerable skepticism about the latter. As one landlady, shrewder than her peers, puts it, "[Y]ou can't always know the Inside by the Outside" (379)—which is only to say that it is very hard to find any language, class or otherwise, that will speak the truth about the human heart. Fielding probably felt that there was some connection between the external sign of class and internal worth. What is most interesting in this novel, however, is the way that Fielding, whatever his class allegiances, shows us how uncertain the connection is between inward value and any of the languages we have formed to express that value.

And the discussion of class inevitably brings us to Blifil, the villain of the piece, whose career in the novel is in every way the dark twin of Tom's, for just as the story traces the revelation of Tom's identity, so it tells the parallel story of the exposure of Blifil's character. Tom, it turns out, is the comic double of the hypocrite: he is a better man than he often seems to be.[9] But Blifil is the real thing. And the problem he represents is largely a linguistic one. Like that of the other great hypocrites in English literature—Chaucer's Pardoner, Spenser's Archimago, Iago, Satan—Blifil's plausibility rests on his skill in using language as a disguise. Milton had summed up the problem well when he called hypocrisy "the only sin that walks / Invisible, except to God alone" (book 3, ll. 683–84), and the cloak of invisibility that the hypocrite wears is almost always made up of words. Blifil's actions—freeing Sophia's bird, for instance, or the look of guilt he betrays when confronted by Allworthy—may reveal the truth of his character, but the force of his words in both cases is sufficient to alter what most of his observers can see. Allworthy has been subject to many readers' abuse for his inability to penetrate Blifil's screen of seeming virtue,[10] but his failures are meant to emphasize his humanity. He may be all-worthy, but he is not divine. Our faith in surfaces, as we saw when we looked at the language of class, our belief that the words we hear have real substance, exercises an almost irresistible pull on our minds, and that pull is often toward disaster. Finally, what separates the tragic from the comic examination of hypocrisy—*Othello*, say, from *Tom Jones*—is whether the discovery of the truth occurs too late or just in time. The best we can do, it seems, is to be plucked from the brink.

After all, Fielding does not want us to rest easy with our privileged knowledge, as readers, of the truth about the "character" of his creations. He admonishes us early on:

> For the Reader is greatly mistaken, if he conceives that *Thwackum* appeared to Mr. *Allworthy* in the same Light as he doth to him in this History; and he is as much deceived, if he imagines, that the most intimate Acquaintance which he himself could have had with that Divine, would have informed him of those Things which we, from our Inspiration, are enabled to open and discover. Of Readers who from such Conceits as these, condemn the Wisdom or Penetration of Mr. *Allworthy*, I shall not scruple to say, that they make a very bad and ungrateful Use of that Knowledge which we have communicated to them. (135)

The narrator here establishes a hierarchy of "penetration"—at the top, himself, guided by "Inspiration" (a clear connection to the divine); then us, the readers, guided by him; and, at the bottom, poor Allworthy, guided by himself alone—an insufficiency, Fielding makes clear, that marks most human activity. Novels, at least those by Henry Fielding, are a very special kind of reading, reading in which we have unaccustomed access to what lurks behind the masks that the villains around us wear.

Yet the novel as a whole quite famously undercuts the alliance of reader and writer affirmed here. In this passage, Fielding insists that *Tom Jones* is "unrealistic," and it is unmimetic simply because we read it too well. Time and again, however, Fielding undermines that assertion as he forces us to acknowledge that our own penetration, even here in this special novelistic world, is as dim as Allworthy's.[11] Indeed, the ending of the novel is delightful in part precisely because we have missed so much along the way. The pleasure we take in rereading *Tom Jones* is made up largely of our new humility, of the rueful joy we take in discovering, from the aesthetic distance of recollection, just where we went wrong.[12] Reading the novel is a "realistic" experience after all: unlike Allworthy, we may know Blifil is bad, but very much like him, we have no idea what the villain is really up to. Here, as in life, we miss a lot.

At work here is a crucial distinction between the failure of reading and what we might call the triumph of writing, between the insufficiency of our ability to understand appearances, to know what we are reading, and the skill of some individuals in creating them. For Fielding, this is not so much a literary issue as it is a moral one, and in order to understand Fielding's thinking on this issue we need to see the way in which he views hypocrisy as both a language and an art. Blifil, in significant ways, is the dark double not only of Tom but of the narrator himself. They do have a lot in common. Both are notorious manipulators, especially given to withholding important information, and as if to emphasize their kinship, what they withhold is often the *same* information, such as Bridget's all-revealing letter to Allworthy. Moreover, both use their linguistic and manipulative skills in order to create plots—the narrator's, wherein Tom is born to be redeemed; and Blifil's, wherein Tom is born to be hanged (Blifil, we note, is always involved whenever there is a criminal accusation against Tom, whether it is the ball he supposedly picks from Blifil's pocket or his "attack" on Fitzgerald). That is, both the narrator and Blifil try to marshal events in order to guarantee certain outcomes. Both are committed, finally, to the world of forms, whether narrative or social. Such an alignment of author and hypocritical character is part of an old tradition. Chaucer exposes the Pardoner, but he never forgets (and never lets us forget) that both he and his creation are storytellers and that stories always stand in an equivocal relation to the truth. Spenser, too, makes Archimago a demonic stand-in for himself, a villain who weaves a bad allegory to compete with and comment on his own. Shakespeare's Iago and Milton's Satan are also artists in this sense, pulled from their creator's brain but never straying too far from his side, reflecting back to him the potential for treachery always inherent in the creative enterprise. Fielding must take his place in this honorable train of self-conscious fabricators. In *Tom Jones*, the effect of the kind of novel-writing competition that takes place between the narrator and Blifil—and we must concede that, while the competition is unfair, Blifil is a good craftsman—is once again to pull us out of complacency and to make us question the truthfulness of any expression that we encounter.[13]

The conclusion Fielding wants us to draw is not that all people are hypocrites but, I believe, that good people and hypocrites may be alike in several ways. This point will be clearer if we look at the vexed issue of "Prudence" in the novel. Battestin has said that prudence is the "dominant ethical theme in the novel,"[14] but the problem for many readers of *Tom Jones* has been to specify what Fielding thinks about this clearly important issue. Here, as in so many other places, Fielding takes away with one hand what he gives with the other. We are told quite early that prudence is the virtue Tom needs to acquire, and at the end, Tom's painfully acquired prudence is loudly celebrated. But we cannot accept these commendations uncritically, for prudence, it turns out, is simultaneously the characteristic of most of the villains in the book, Blifil above all. Prudence is a necessary virtue, but it is also the kind of duplicitous discretion that someone like Blifil seems to have at his effortless command. Battestin is at learned pains to distinguish between two kinds of prudence—the proper variety, which is a kind of "practical wisdom," and the villainous brand, which is a dangerous "counterfeit" of such wisdom and nothing more than "cunning."[15] The relation of such false prudence to hypocrisy is clear: both create a counterfeit image. But many readers are left uneasy with this distinction. Why should Fielding use the same word to describe morally opposing qualities?

If we return to the assumption that has governed this discussion so far, that Fielding's central concern in *Tom Jones* is to examine skeptically all forms of human expression, then we should find it fruitful to think of prudence itself as a kind of language. Indeed, this is precisely what Fielding wants us to do. Let us look carefully at the passage in which the narrator commends prudence as the quality young Tom most urgently needs to acquire:

In recording some Instances [of Tom's wildness], we shall, if rightly understood, afford a very useful Lesson to those well-disposed Youths, who shall hereafter be our Readers: For they may here find that Goodness of Heart, and Openness of Temper, tho' these may give them great Comfort within, and administer to an honest Pride in their own Minds, will by no Means, alas! do their Business in the World. Prudence and Circumspection are necessary even to the best of Men. They are indeed as it were a Guard to Virtue, without which she can never be safe. It is not enough that your Designs, nay that your Actions are intrinsically good, you must take Care that they shall appear so. If your Inside be never so beautiful, you must preserve a fair Outside also. This must be constantly looked to, or Malice and Envy will take Care to blacken it so, that the Sagacity and Goodness of an *Allworthy* will not be able to see through it, and to discern the Beauties within. Let this, my young Readers, be your constant Maxim, That no Man can be good enough to enable him to neglect the Rules of Prudence; nor will Virtue herself look beautiful, unless she be bedecked with the outward Ornaments of Decency and Decorum. (141)

This passage has a worldly tone that verges on world-weariness, even cynicism—a reminder that ethics and pragmatics are often closely yoked in Fielding's mind. The implications need to be drawn out at some length. What we can note first is the pervasive language of inner and outer; there is the "intrinsic" and the apparent, the "Inside" and the "outside," "Beauties within" and "outward Ornaments." The key phrase is perhaps *see through*, an action presented here (predictably enough, in light of what we have seen) as a failure. *Tom Jones* is stuffed with examples of bad reading, and poor Allworthy's "Sagacity and Goodness," we are almost gratuitously reminded, are not enough to make a difference. The fundamental assumption here is that there is no *necessary* connection between the interior self—that world of thought, feeling, and motivation I have called character—and the forms, or identity, by which that world is expressed. Good people do not always look good; bad ones often appear just fine. The mien is the message that we receive, but the mien, itself a language, may have nothing to do with the truth. Yet the situation is actually worse than this: a law of entropy governs, and if we leave things to themselves, between carelessness and the calumny of villains, the good person will generally look bad. We could say, then, that the burden of responsibility, to return to my earlier distinction, is on the writer, not the reader—not, that is, on the one who reads the text of the self but on the one who writes it. Hence, Fielding's string of admonitions: "must take care," "must preserve," "must be constantly looked to." The urgency of the vocabulary suggests how real the danger of being misread is.

Morality here is inseparable from language and from art. The good person must find a form or language to express inward character, but that construction of an accurately legible identity is, we note, an aestheticized process—what the virtuous must do is to "ornament" and "bedeck" themselves to create an appearance at once beautiful and truthful. But the beauty we see in virtue is always painfully constructed, and it may be nothing more than a lie, for the problem, as we have seen, is that the villain is a rival artist, always threatening to "blacken" the canvas that goodness presents to the world and to create his own beautiful surface. We observe that in this passage both the virtuous individual and the villain "take Care"—their labor is much the same; only the ends are different. One struggles prudently to craft an exterior image that matches inward worth; the other labors—also prudently—to create a surface picture that will mask interior flaws. But both are artificers. There is no "natural" language or expression of virtue, at least no reliable one. All expressions—of affection, of status, of goodness—are artificial. The only difference—and it is of course important—is whether one has used artifice to reveal or to hide the truth of the self, but the tools of the good-natured human being are the same as those of the hypocrite.

In an eighteenth-century context, artificiality is not necessarily a bad thing, for the spontaneous overflow of powerful emotion, as Tom demonstrates, produces much trouble and no poetry at all. But without imposing anachronistic romantic values on Fielding's world, there remains a lingering subversiveness in the novel's discussion of prudence. The problem is not what Johnson feared—that Fielding creates characters in whom good and bad qualities are mixed;[16] rather, Fielding shows us both kinds of people occupied in the same way, in fashioning a self. As we saw with his explorations of sexuality and class, Fielding does not want to deny hierarchies of value, and Battestin is probably right to say that there is good and bad prudence, just as there is good and bad love. But the author of *Tom Jones* seems more interested in examining the problems inherent in the expression and apprehension of these hierarchies than in describing the nature of human worth and villainy. That is, he is concerned less about Tom's goodness or Blifil's flaws than about why those qualities are so difficult for most people to recognize. And the blame is widespread: people, in general, read badly the many kinds of language they encounter; Tom expresses himself poorly, Blifil, all too well; language itself, in whatever form, often seems less various than the truths it is called on to express.

Such a summary fails to acknowledge that *Tom Jones* is a specifically comic masterpiece. Fielding plucks us, as well as Tom, from the precipice, and we revel in a conclusion of universal happiness. Everyone gets married (even the exiled Blifil is on the verge), the truth about everything emerges, and we put down the book with a smile. Providence in the form of a narrator has made all come right. For some readers, that narrative providence means we can read analagously upward and conclude that a benevolent God exerts a similar control over the ultimate shape of human life.[17] Perhaps. But I do not believe that Fielding wants us, in our rush to savor the novel's comic apocalypse, to leave behind the bracing—even, at times, sobering—skepticism whose value he has made so apparent all along. "Truth," whatever that may be, is real and it has triumphed here, but it remains hard to see. At the end of *Tom Jones*, in the little world that Fielding has created, everyone gets lucky, but such luck as we see occurs in spite of the treachery of language. Our own fate may not be so secure.

4

Tristram Shandy:
The Laughter of Feeling

In the novels we have looked at so far, the didactic intentions of the writers have always been clear, if not always successful. Defoe insisted that Crusoe's adventures had a "religious Application" and should lead people to "justify and honour the Wisdom of Providence" (1); Richardson claimed that he wanted to "investigate the highest and most important Doctrines not only of Morality, but of Christianity" (1: xx); and even the urbane Fielding said that his "sincere Endeavour" in *Tom Jones* was "to recommend Goodness and Innocence" (7). For these writers, the novel form seemed perfectly suited to one of the eighteenth century's most revered aesthetic ideals: the Horatian *dulce et utile,* or the idea that instruction can appropriately be delivered in the guise of an entertainment. For the early novelists, narrative itself was, almost by definition, entertaining. But it should also serve higher ends, and such higher ends—morality, religion, goodness—were indeed what these writers believed they were serving. Laurence Sterne appropriates this tradition but does so very much to his own ends. For him, *dulce* is *utile:* the sweetness is not a coating on the pill of instruction but the medicine itself. The author of *Tristram Shandy* insists that his work is not a vehicle for a lesson; rather, his novel is valuable simply because it is entertaining. As Sterne says in the book's dedication, he lives and writes "in a constant endeavour to fence against the infirmities of ill-health, and other evils of life, by mirth; being firmly persuaded that every time a man smiles—but much more so, when he laughs, that it adds something to this Fragment of Life."[1] Sterne's claim here is odd in at least two ways. First, he has apparently abandoned the traditional moral intentions (hence justifications for writing) of his predecessors. The second, less apparent oddity is his specific recommendation of the salubrious power of laughter. The peculiarity of Sterne's promotion of laughter cannot be fully appreciated unless we understand the place of laughter in his own culture.

For a modern observer, eighteenth-century England represents a curious moment in the history of laughter. It was an age that produced some of the finest comic writing and some of the greatest wits that England has known, and that often seemed to find the most characteristic and successful expression of its genius in satire. Yet *laughter*, as opposed to comedy or wit (and the distinction is crucial), seems to have had an equivocal status. In *The Lives of the Poets*, Dr. Johnson tells us that neither Pope nor Swift was ever seen to laugh,[2] and Chesterfield, in 1748, in one of his celebrated letters to his son, cautioned the latter against laughing in revealing terms, calling it "the manner in which the mob express their silly joy at silly things" and adding that "since I had full use of my reason, nobody has ever heard me laugh."[3] Descriptions of human behavior are typically so saturated with ideology that it is probably unwise to take such statements at face value. Did the man who imagined a projector trying to extract sunbeams from cucumbers really *never* laugh? In any event, it is more revealing to see how people of another time represented themselves than to worry too much about what they actually did, which is not recoverable outside such representations anyway. And the assumption seems to have been among many, including the witty, that laughter was unseemly, vulgar, or (in a word they might have used) "low."

Quite another explanation for these attitudes toward laughter can be found in the middle of the preceding century, in the very famous comments on laughter proposed by that notorious anatomizer of the frailties of human nature, Thomas Hobbes. He described laughter as "a distortion of the countenance" and claimed that it is "nothing else but *sudden glory* arising from some sudden *conception* of some *eminency* in ourselves, by *comparison* with the *infirmity* of others, or with our own formerly" (his italics).[4] That is, laughter is an expression of a sense of power in ourselves, and it is easy to surmise that the resistance to laughter among the members of the Scriblerus Club or in a snob like Chesterfield is rooted in an attempt to evince implacable self-assurance. If we laugh when we suddenly (a word Hobbes repeats twice) are aware of our potency in comparison with someone else, then the clear implication is that most people usually lack any firm or continued sense of self-confidence and command. The "silly" rabble, lacking such assurance, gratefully and gleefully clings with laughter to whatever "silly things" can temporarily alleviate their position and provide them with that fragile feeling of superiority.

If there was pressure in the eighteenth century to suppress laughter as vulgar, there was also repression from certain religious elements. Puritan suspicion of frivolity was long established, and at midcentury the new members of the enthusiastic ranks, the Methodists, reenergized the religious condemnation of laughter by exhorting adherents to "avoid all lightness as you would hell-fire, and laughing as you would cursing and swearing."[5] Thus, it is against this background—laughter as low or laughter as sinful—that we must try to understand and appreciate the laughter of Laurence Sterne, gentleman, Cambridge graduate, clergyman.

Fielding, Sterne's intellectual and artistic godfather in many ways and himself a good friend to laughter, is different in this regard, as different as comedy is from laughter. Comedy, we might say, is primarily a matter of form (patterns of rebirth or ascent, happy endings) and value (order, justice, love); laughter neither includes nor excludes those considerations but is best seen as something separate, as a behavior, response, or attitude or as an alternative mode of expression to the discourse of words. It is difficult to analyze *Tristram Shandy* as a comedy in any useful formal sense of that term. But then, it does not want to be a comedy—what it wants to do is to make us laugh. That is its palpable design upon us. And Sterne has proceeded in this way for the simple reason that he believes that laughter is good for us, that it is quite literally a source of good health. His book, he says, "if 'tis wrote against any thing,—'tis wrote, an' please your worships, against the spleen; in order, by a more frequent and a more convulsive elevation and depression of the diaphragm, and the succussations of the intercostal and abdominal muscles in laughter, to drive the *gall* and other *bitter juices* from the gall bladder, liver, and sweet-bread of his majesty's subjects, with all the inimicitious passions which belong to them, down into their duodenums" (360).

It is, of course, a risky business to focus on a writer's intentions, especially so in the case of Sterne, who constantly thwarts the expectations he has aroused in very deliberate ways. It perhaps follows from that tendency that a great many twentieth-century commentators on Sterne appear to have determined, on a kind of principle of inversion, that Sterne (an appropriate name for the writer they are reading) is not a jester but a very serious writer indeed. For these critics, Arnold was right. Literary greatness requires high seriousness, and Sterne passes the test with honors. As

Richard Lanham puts it, in his excellent summary of the history of
Sterne criticism, for many modern readers Sterne "reenacts existential philosophy, confronting absurdity with a jest, but preoccupied,
finally, with the most serious problems, the most fundamental issues."[6] In a crucial sense, such critics restore Sterne to the Horatian
ideal: what is entertaining in his novel, perhaps covertly but always powerfully, actually does serve as a vehicle for admirably
weighty instruction. In this light, *Tristram Shandy* emerges as a
mainstream eighteenth-century work after all. What I want to do in
this chapter, however, is—very cautiously—take Sterne at his
word. What does it mean to say that laughter really is the end that
he is striving to achieve?

It is possible that the temptation to make Sterne solemn arises
from that side of humor which is inherently intellectual. The dual
connotations of "wit"—intelligence and humor—are no accident.
At the same time, we must again remind ourselves of the difference
between wit and laughter. Laughter, as distinct from wit, exists, we
might say, at the intersection of nature and culture; our ability to
laugh is closely bound to our distinctive cultural capacities of intelligence and language. But we must also remember that laughter,
whatever inspires it, remains an *embodied* response, one that is like
language in that it is a meaningful expression but one that is nonetheless nonverbal and, above all, bodily. The refusal to laugh by the
Scriblerians or by Chesterfield may in part be an attempt to deny
this ambiguity, but Sterne, I believe, embraces it; he relishes the
possibility that in laughter our natural and cultural identities converge and—briefly, anyway—are reconciled. Thus, as the foregoing
passages suggest, what Sterne wants is a belly laugh, a laugh that
may be inspired by wit but is finally both from and for the body, a
laughter that is not only the product of intelligence but also the
promoter of good feeling. But "feelings," like laughter, are a concept with a particular freight of meaning in eighteenth-century England, and we must pause to consider the possible relation of
Sterne's laughter to his role in that tradition called sensibility.

That tradition is usually connected with not laughter but tears. In
reaction to the rationalist stance of the Age of Enlightenment and
encouraged by the inherent subjectivity of Lockean epistemology
and the benevolent ideas of human nature advanced by Shaftes-
bury and the latitudinarians, what is often called a cult of feeling
emerged in the middle of the eighteenth century. Our distinctive

humanity, it was thought, resided in our capacity for emotion, particularly in sympathetic identification with the plight of others. In turn, the awareness of these feelings confirmed humanity's essential goodness, and tears thus became an eloquent sign of the generous heart.[7]

The relation between this tradition and the century's new form, the novel, is not at all simple, as two prominent examples illustrate. Richardson is often considered one of the high priests of the movement and appropriately so, in light of his intense focus on the feelings of his characters and his masterful ability to inspire sympathetic identification with their sufferings among his readers. When Clarissa died, a nation wept. At the same time, Richardson's work—which, as Diderot said, carried the torch to the back of the cave of human motivation and revealed the "hideous Moor" that lurked therein—can hardly be considered (to borrow Hazlitt's description of Uncle Toby) a compliment to human nature.[8] Indeed, in the postscript to *Clarissa,* arguing against those who begged him to end the novel happily, Richardson begins to attack his readers in an extraordinary way, claiming that the champions of a happy ending did not want him to eliminate Clarissa's suffering altogether, "for the sake of the sport her distresses would give to the tender-hearted reader as she went along" (4: 552). This stance is a little like a pornographer berating his audience for becoming aroused, but it also strongly points to Richardson's deep ambivalence about the meaning of the sensibility he tapped. For him, suffering is not "sport" or a sign of human goodness; it is a reminder that we live in a fallen world. Fielding, on the other hand, despite his wealth of devices for distancing us from the action and for thwarting the kind of ego dissolve so characteristic of Richardson's readers, seems firmly within the benevolent and latitudinarian frame of thought.[9] We know that Tom Jones is good (in the same way that we recognize all of Fielding's good characters) precisely because of his capacity for feeling and especially for spontaneous sympathy.

Sterne has always had the reputation of being one of the central figures in the sensibility movement, and near the end of *A Sentimental Journey* he breaks into a panegyric that is arguably the classic statement of the doctrine: "Dear sensibility! source inexhausted of all that's precious in our joys, or costly in our sorrows! . . .—eternal fountain of our feelings! . . . [T]his is the divinity which stirs within

me— . . . that I feel some generous cares beyond myself—all comes
from thee, great, great SENSORIUM of the world!"[10] The allusion,
however, to Milton here—when Adam eats the apple, he and Eve
feel "Divinity within them" (book 9, l. 1010)—usefully reminds us
that Sterne, like Richardson and Fielding, should not be seen as any
simple or univocal spokesman for sensibility. The echo suggests
that sympathy is perhaps as illusory as Adam and Eve's exhilara-
tion. But with this warning in mind, it is still clear that sensibility is
one train of thought that has left its imprint on *Tristram Shandy*. In
fact, if the Victorian readers had had their way, the novel would
have been reduced to a bowdlerized anthology of sentimental
moments—Uncle Toby's heartwarming befuddlements, the death
of Le Fever, and so on. Such an anthology, we should note, would
be fairly brief in comparison to the novel that we have, which is
made up far more of jokes than of tearful interludes. Accordingly, I
would like to look at Sterne's "sensibility" (in the sense of both
temperament and ideology) in another way. Laughter, as we have
seen, should make us feel good. Can those good feelings be related
to the kind of good feelings Sterne praises in the address to sensibility quoted earlier? Is there such a thing as sentimental laughter, a
laughter of feeling?

We should probably distinguish at the outset of this discussion
between a writer's representation of laughter (which is a matter of
characterization) and his or her creation of laughter (a matter of
reader response). These occasions may be the same, as when we as
readers laugh along with a character or characters, or they may be
separate. The representation of laughter in the eighteenth century
is often clearly Hobbesian: the king of Brobdingnag laughs loud
and long at Gulliver's tale of the greatness of England; Lovelace
sets aside his pen, he tells Belford, to laugh at the spectacle of the
paragon Clarissa running away from her family; and even the ten-
derhearted Tom Jones must laugh at the sight of the philosopher
Square hidden amongst the "other female Utensils" of Molly's attic
room. In all these instances, someone in the narrative is being
laughed at, and the one who laughs does so from a feeling of
personal power—Hobbes's "sudden glory." Such a Hobbesian element, we will see, is not missing from *Tristram Shandy*. But even
more striking, initially anyway, is the fact that the representation of
laughter is itself largely missing from this work. We know that
Tristram is a lover of laughter, but we do not see him laughing,

perhaps because so much of the "action" of the book takes place before he is born. As John Preston points out, a great deal of the narrative consists of the conversation of Walter and Toby, neither of whom is much given to laughter.[11] In fact, at one moment when Walter shows his sharpest wit, significantly enough, he weeps:

> My mother and my uncle *Toby* expected my father would be the death of *Obidiah*—and that there never would be an end of the disaster.—See here! you rascal, cried my father, pointing to the mule, what you have done!—It was not me, said *Obidiah*.—How do I know that? replied my father.
>
> Triumph swam in my father's eyes, at the repartee—the *Attic* salt brought water into them—and so *Obidiah* heard no more about it. (420–21)

The scene should be perfectly Hobbesian—Walter's witty triumph at the expense of the hapless Obidiah—but the victor here does not laugh, nor does he retain an Augustan composure. He cries instead. Yet we can hardly call these "sympathetic" tears, and Sterne is not here portraying any moment of human connection such as the devotees of sensibility worshiped. Nonetheless, the air of sensibility implied by the tears is present, for in the moment of his glory Walter does forget Obidiah's crime, and while the forgiveness may be inadvertent, it is real enough for Obidiah, who had, seconds before, been facing no "end of the disaster."

Wit and tears, solitary triumph and human forgiveness are all oddly mixed in this episode, and that kind of ambivalence is characteristic of the humor of *Tristram Shandy*. Walter's tears are a kind of stand-in here for the laughter Sterne has commended as health giving: the repartee has made him not so much laugh or cry as feel better. And such a substitution serves to remind us that what Sterne appears to want most is what I have called a laughter of feeling. If it is not precisely from the heart, nonetheless it does the heart good. That, in turn, suggests the particular dialectic of laughter and feeling that Sterne establishes throughout. What this incident suggests and what we will see again and again are that Sterne does not really reject the Hobbesian analysis of the source of laughter but in large measure is able to transvalue the Hobbesian description of the effects of laughter. For Hobbes, laughter reinforces the reality of hierarchy—the one who laughs is always above the object—and thus such laughter ultimately reminds us of the Hobbesian description of existence itself, the struggle to survive in a world where life is solitary, nasty, brutish, and short. Sterne, as a scene like this illustrates, does not really deny the inequality at the heart of humor, nor does he fundamentally disagree with Hobbes's sense of the brutal facts of existence. But "sudden glory" is not the end of the story, even if it is the beginning. Walter's good feeling may originate in his glory at one man's expense, but ultimately and ironically, everyone feels better.

Since we see so little laughter represented in the novel, what we must look for are the moments when Sterne wants us to laugh. And my emphasis in the following discussion will be not so much on techniques as effects. To what end does Sterne make us laugh, what is his design upon us, and above all, why does his brand of laughter make us feel better? What I want to suggest is that Sterne's laughter, as Hobbes says, usually does involve power but that the inequality that Hobbes emphasizes, the sense that every scene of laughter has a winner and a loser, dissolves. The "glory" of Shandean laughter is not power over others but power over everything that can be subsumed under the capacious rubric of mortality.

Of course, Hobbes's is not the only model of laughter available to us, though it does have the virtue of historical proximity. The sensibility movement can be considered, among other things, as an attempt to refute Hobbes,[12] and if we see Sterne as holding down the job of Minister for Laughter in the sentimental cabinet, Hobbes's model is a good place to begin a description of his job. There is, however, another model, less contemporary but in many ways more revealing about Sterne. I have in mind Mikhail Bakhtin's "carnival laughter" as he describes it in *Rabelais and His World*.[13] Carnival laughter is a specifically medieval phenomenon, and Bakhtin is at some pains to distinguish its moment in the history of laughter from later developments, especially those beginning in the eighteenth century, when, he insists, the carnival spirit is rejected in the face of a dominant classical aesthetic. In fact, Bakhtin singles Sterne out as an exemplar of a new subjectivity at midcentury, a privacy of vision completely at odds with the community Bakhtin perceives in the carnivalesque. As he puts it, in the eighteenth century, "laughter loses its essential link with a universal outlook" (101). While acknowledging the force of his insistence that laughter has a history, and keeping in mind that we ignore historical distinctions at our peril, I also believe that the concept of carnival laughter is useful for understanding *Tristram Shandy*. In the first place, Rabelais himself, whose work, according to Bakhtin, is the pinnacle of the carnivalesque, is one of Sterne's own models and masters. Moreover, Bakhtin notes that the older forms of laughter did persist in new or less canonical genres like the novel (102). Let me hasten to add here that *Tristram Shandy* is not the product of the spirit of medieval folk humor; nevertheless, I do believe that such humor can illuminate Sterne's novel, historically distant as it is from the model Bakhtin has elaborated.

According to Bakhtin, carnival laughter (the phrase is his) is marked by three primary characteristics. First, it is "the laughter of all the people," or, as he puts it later, a product of "the social consciousness of all the people" (11, 92). Second, "it is universal in scope," by which he (unlike Hobbes) means that it does not sharply distinguish between those who laugh and those who are laughed at; the laughter *includes* the participants (11–12). Finally, it is "ambivalent"—it "asserts and denies, it buries and revives" (11–12). Such ambivalence creates an emphasis on what Bakhtin calls "grotesque realism," an aesthetic that comprehends the interdependence of life and death. By concentrating always on the sense of becoming, such an aesthetic therefore rejects whatever seems finished or complete. At the heart of this conception of the grotesque is that it must be the "epitome of incompleteness" (18–26). In sum, then, carnival laughter is communal, universal, and ambivalent; above all, it erodes distinctions—between people and between life and death. And as an eroding force, it inevitably represents a challenge to authority, and Bakhtin makes much of the contrast between the laughing world of the carnival and the solmen "official" world of church and state. As he puts it, the carnivalesque "celebrated . . . liberation from . . . prevailing truth . . . and established order" (10).

Before discussing the usefulness of these ideas for Sterne, it is best to concede the ways in which they do not work. Bakhtin explicitly labels *Tristram Shandy* the "first important example of the new subjective grotesque," an "individualistic world outlook very different from the carnival folk concept of previous ages" (36). Certainly it is difficult to see Sterne's laughter as "communal" in the way Bakhtin describes the original carnivalesque. The experience of reading Sterne's novel is, as almost every reader has noticed, an encounter with the isolation of individual consciousness.

Along with many others in the middle of the eighteenth century, Sterne recognized that Lockean psychology did not really affirm the existence of a shared reality but, rather, opened the door to an inescapably subjective epistemology. As Sterne himself puts it, "I will tell you in three words what the book [Locke's *Essay concerning Human Understanding*] is.—It is a history-book, Sir, (which may possibly recommend it to the world) of what passes in a man's own mind" (98). And what passes in a man's own mind is pretty much his own, very private business—Walter's theories, Toby's sieges, Tristram's opinions. The hobbyhorse is many things in *Tristram Shandy*—a source of amusement for others, a cure for one's own quotidian cares—but most of all, perhaps, it is an expression of each man's singularity, a mark that sets each of us apart from our fellows. Sterne recognizes that, in the wake of Locke, we are all alone, and that our attempts to communicate across that gulf separating one consciousness from another are finally doomed. Language in particular, the "unsteady uses of words" (100), can only lead astray. When Toby tells the widow Wadman that she "shall lay [her] finger upon the place" where he got his wound, Sterne dryly comments on the ensuing misunderstanding, "It shews what little knowledge is got by mere words" (773).

Sterne, though, is not in despair about this isolation, and his commitment to sensibility has long been singled out as the answer he offers to the potential prison of subjectivity. As Max Byrd puts it, "Subjectivity yields only to sentiment."[14] Can it yield to laughter as well, especially if Sterne's brand of laughter, as Bakhtin contends, is already implicated in the very subjectivity it wishes to erase? Bakhtin says that the laughter of the "Romantic grotesque" (an aesthetic that he says is "founded" by Sterne) was "cut down to cold humor, irony, sarcasm. It ceased to be joyful and triumphant hilarity. Its positive regenerating power was reduced to a minimum" (37–38). In this light, Sterne's is nothing but a Hobbesian laughter: philosophical subjectivism has blended with the pleasure of individual triumph to produce a laughter that is solitary indeed. But I am not sure about Bakhtin's analysis of Sterne. Even if we concede the subjectivity of *Tristram Shandy* and jettison the possibility that Sterne's laughter can be "communal" in the same way as medieval folk humor, I think we can still see in the other two characteristics of that humor—its universality and its ambivalence—ways to understand better the laughter of Laurence Sterne, and especially ways to free it from the cold and brutal world of Hobbes. If we can do that, then we can comprehend why Sterne thought his laughter was health and life giving, how it could serve as a force of "regeneration" and as a bridge to human connection.

I will begin with ambivalence. As we have seen, ambivalent laughter celebrates the incompleteness of existence and constantly forces us to confront the interpenetration of life and death. Ambivalent laughter manages to be both "gay" and "mocking, deriding" (12). And the ambivalent laughter of *Tristram Shandy* shows up nowhere more clearly than in its treatment of sex and death. These two forces, of course, provide the basis of most narrative form. Stories have to end somewhere, and marriage and death are the typical occasions for narrative closure. We could say, following Huizinga, that there are two possible "rules" for determining when the narrative "game" is over, for a game by definition must have such a rule.[15] Sterne, suffering as he is from a terminal case of tuberculosis, sees in his story and its serial publication (the nine volumes were published in five parts over about seven years) the sign of his continued life. Accordingly, his desire is to create a narrative without a rule of closure. That way, as he says, it will "be kept a-going these forty years, if it pleases the fountain of health to bless me so long with life and good spirits" (82). The implication is clear, however, that he means just the opposite of what he says: his unending book is itself his fountain of health; it is his novel that will supply him with life and keep him going. Therefore, as an author who is writing his own life-support system, he must tread very carefully around the subjects of sex and death in order to thwart the possible eruption of any principle of narrative closure whatsoever. The well-known catalog of sexual impotence and frustration in the novel—Toby's wound in the groin, Tristram's bungled delivery and accidental "circumcision," the incapable bull, and so on—are thus ironically meant to serve as signs of continued life. The little death of orgasm, of any sexual completion, is too uncomfortably close to the final death awaiting us all, and the avoidance of the former may—somehow—postpone the latter. It is quite a ridiculous assumption, and in response we have to laugh, an ambivalent laughter that comprehends at once the facts that, from the point of view of the species, sex is the only answer to death and that, from the perspective of the individual, it is finally no answer at all. As I see it, this is the heart of ambivalent laughter: sex makes us laugh because it celebrates life and because it simultaneously reminds us that the attempt to avoid death is finally futile. Sexual laughter is both triumphant and derisive, joyfully vital yet tinged with death.

To illustrate this point more fully, let us look in some detail at the opening chapters of volume 1. Because *Tristram Shandy* is blatantly uncommitted to narrative progress, it is a book that, more so than most novels, is best considered in small pieces—as its original serial publication implies. To try to read through it in the way that novels usually encourage is to come face to face with the dread warning Dr. Johnson carved over the entrance to *Clarissa*, words true enough for Richardson but even more accurate for Sterne: "If you were to read Richardson for the story, your impatience would be so much fretted that you would hang yourself."[16] The attempt to read Sterne wholesale is probably what lies behind Cyril Connolly's judgment that reading *Tristram Shandy* reminds him of a child trying to see how slowly he can ride a bicycle without falling off.[17] I suspect that Sterne's happiest readers are those who have the luxury of savoring him a few chapters at a time. I proceed, then, with the assumption that not only can we usefully generalize about the whole by scrutinizing a small part but the consideration of too much Sterne at one time may enfeeble us as readers and make us less receptive than we usually are.

The first five chapters of *Tristram Shandy*, covering only about six pages, recount the moment of Tristram's conception. The scene is remarkably rich with implications, both for this book and for narrative generally. The first question we must ask is, Why does Sterne begin here? The answer is both biographical and literary: this conception narrative apparently answers both "where did I come from?" and "Where do I start?" As we will see, however, the naive faith in origins implied in this "begin at the beginning" attitude is thoroughly demolished by the scene itself. The opening of the novel exposes itself quickly as inadequate, both as the beginning of the story and as an explanation for the origin of Tristram's personality. At the same time, it is a perfect evocation in miniature of the form and content of the entire novel.

First, in many ways this is a beginning in which nothing is begun. We do not have to read far to discover that this particular March night in 1718 has almost nothing to do with the action (such as it is) of the novel, and large chunks of the story will recount—with, of course, perfect eyewitness accuracy—events that took place long before either Tristram's conception or his birth. More-over, Sterne goes to considerable pains to cast doubt on Tristram's certainty that this was actually the night on which he was con-ceived. After twice emphasizing that pregnancy is a nine-month process, Tristram tells us that he was in fact born almost exactly eight months after the scene he has described. As if to underline our doubts, he protests that this is a period "as near nine kalendar months as any husband could in reason have expected" (8). We immediately doubt both the accuracy of Tristram's decision to be-gin here and the fidelity of Mrs. Shandy, since we also learn that, by reason of a "Sciatica" (7), Walter was incapable of performing his nuptial duties for three months prior to the night in question. Like Tom Jones's, Tristram's conception is apparently missing; un-like Fielding, however, Sterne will never fill that narrative gap with better information.

But if this was not the night on which Tristram was conceived, and especially if Walter was not Tristram's father, then the ag-grieved tone that opens the novel is totally inappropriate: "I Wish either my father or my mother, or indeed both of them, as they were in duty both equally bound to it, had minded what they were about when they begot me; . . .—Had they duly weighed and con-sidered all this, and proceeded accordingly,—I am verily per-suaded I should have made a quite different figure in the world, from that, in which the reader is likely to see me" (1). The event that Tristram considers to be the origin of both his life and his troubles (which in turn produce the "opinions" that are his other, ostensible subject) may thus be the origin of nothing. And the dubiety the scene inspires in the reader goes even deeper if we step back and ask, How does Tristram know all this? What we have here, after all, is no ordinary primal scene in which a child must somehow retroactively connect the action before him with his own origin. Tristram instead seems to be a witness to his own begetting, can apparently answer yes to Satan's troubling question that we looked at in an earlier chapter, "Remember'st thou thy making?" And we receive no satisfaction when we learn that Tristram does have a source for all this information, namely, his uncle Toby, to whom he claims to be "indebted for the preceding anecdote," which Toby, in turn, got from Walter (4). It is a preposterous idea to think that Toby, whose innocence in matters sexual could rival that of an anchorite, would "under[stand] . . . very well" (4) what Walter was telling him. Any story about the origin of a child that comes from Toby has all the authority of a tale about storks or cabbage patches.

By now, whatever sense we might have had that this incident has the authority to explain or begin anything has totally evaporated. Yet Sterne will not let us abandon it, for if circumstantial evidence suggests that Walter may not be Tristram's father and therefore that the son's complaint against the father as the source of his woes is misplaced, what we must concede, on the other hand, is how thoroughly like old Walter Tristram is—a likeness that manifests itself precisely in these complaints. In the opening scene, Tristram launches into a complex explanation of the fragility of the homunculus and the tragic dispersion of animal spirits that accompanied the impregnating journey of his own "little Gentleman" (3). Yet we learn almost immediately that such etiological speculation is not original to Tristram but is an inheritance from Walter, who with a tear in his eye explains that *"My Tristram's misfortunes began nine months before ever he came into the world"* (4). Of course, since this incident occurred *eight* months before Tristram's arrival, we can hardly be said to have found solid ground here. Nonetheless, what is clear is that the opinions of the father have been visited upon the son. The theory of the origin of his troubles that we thought was Tristram's turns out to be Walter's. Reproduction is a mysterious business in *Tristram Shandy;* think not only of the uncertainty here, but of that mule whose unexpected appearance so angers Walter. But if conception emerges as a dubious explanation of origins, in some way reproduction has still occurred, and from the start of the novel we know that the son has taken the father's image. That is not to say that Tristram is a replica of Walter, because he is not, but the coincidence of opinion here suggests that some discernible part of the spirit that animates Tristram did originate in his father and that this speculative old man has reproduced himself in a way that we can recognize.

My discussion of this scene has so far avoided what might be considered its most essential feature, as well as its funniest aspect. The homunculus that would be Tristram is so traumatized on its journey because, at the crucial moment, Mrs. Shandy (whose role in the novel is cameo and whose most memorable appearance is here) asks, *"Pray, my dear . . . have you not forgot to wind up the clock?"* (2). *Tristram Shandy* begins with an act of coitus interruptus, and if that event is, as we have seen, problematic as an explanation of the origin of Tristram, it will turn out to be more than adequate as a description of the origin of this book. It is an originating act in several important ways. Mrs. Shandy's query, based on Walter's regular performance of two household tasks on the same evening of every month, establishes from the outset the kind of comic Lockean associations, those "strange combination[s] of ideas" (7), that will permeate the text. This interruption is also only the first of many, and what Sterne establishes at the outset is a narrative pattern based on sexual frustration. In *Tristram Shandy*, neither stories nor sex has a beginning, a middle, and an end. Apparently taking his license from the fact that our sexual terminology tends to mirror the way we describe stories, Sterne creates a narrative aesthetic based not on the inevitable climax (which even a marathoner like Richardson eventually delivers) but on digression and delay. Yet we must consider further the relation of sex and time.

Sexual union is ideally atemporal; as Eve tells Adam, "With thee conversing I forget all time." Coitus interruptus implies the premature reappearance of temporality (and its attendant, mortality), and Mrs. Shandy's ill-timed question seems a perfect expression of the return of the temporarily suspended sense of time. Do not forget time, she says, do not forget death. The clock has stopped, and it is Walter's duty to wind it, to make time proceed. But the image of sexually suspended time is, for the Shandys, ludicrous. We remember that this particular "strange combination of ideas" has become established because Walter had brought several "little family concernments" together in order "to get them all out of the way at one time, and be no more plagued and pester'd with them the rest of the month" (6). That is, sex has become a chore, and as part of the routine it is, far from being atemporal, merely another marker of time's progress. Mrs. Shandy thus inverts Eve: "conversing" with Walter, the clock is all she can think about. But if the clock never stops for them and if sex is only a reminder of time's encroaching and mortally progressive power in the Shandys' life, the interruption represents something else for us. As readers, we are able to enjoy a moment outside time, the moment in which we laugh. The interruption of climax, it turns out, whatever its consequences for Tristram and his parents, is the moment of our reward, because for us then, the clock *is* temporarily stopped. Our laughter in that moment between tick and tock is deeply ambivalent. We laugh because the futility of both the Shandys' and our own attempts to escape death is exposed, and we laugh because, as we saw earlier, the interruption of completion is simultaneously and ironically a temporary defeat of time. For Sterne, coitus interruptus is a paradox—it is an image of death and, quite literally, of misbegotten life, but it is also a joke on death, a refusal of teleology, since teleology can never define itself without an end.

There is yet another way to look at the opening pages of *Tristram Shandy*, one I suggested earlier when I referred to them as a primal scene. According to the classical Freudian understanding of this early trauma, the child, in witnessing directly the sexuality of its parents, is forced quite brutally to confront the reality of its own oedipal defeat. Ernest Becker's reinterpretation of this doctrine proves as useful here as it did when we looked at *Robinson Crusoe*. For Becker, the primal scene is the moment when the child faces its own mortality, when it learns, as we saw in that chapter, that it was made and did not make itself.[18] For Freudians, that experience of contingency is so painful that we must repress the knowledge, and, as we saw, *Crusoe* represents one of the most powerful fantasies of denial of this truth ever created. In light of Bakhtin's views, however, the primal scene can be experienced in another way, as the ultimate inspiration to ambivalent laughter. The knowledge of our own making, which Tristram seems to have so directly and which he shows no signs of repressing, is an experience of the final indissolubility of life and death. In his knowledge of his conception, Tristram sees his life, and in the comic exaggerations and frustrations that attend that conception, he sees more legibly than usual the truth that is always implicit in the creation of new life, the reality of death. In conceiving life, we also and inevitably conceive death, and there is no help for that final irony except laughter.

Freud, of course, is another theoretician of laughter, and it would be useful to pause a moment to consider his remarks on humor in light of the model I have been developing here. Bakhtin scrupulously avoids any mention of Freud, an omission that seems particularly curious given the importance of "ambivalence" in Bakhtin's scheme—Freud actually coined that word so central to the thinking of both men. The crucial difference between them is their attitude toward history. Bakhtin, as we have seen, wants to write a history of laughter, and for a mind as ahistorical as Freud's, the idea of a history of laughter would probably be as strange as a history of sexuality. The fact that such histories have now been—and continue to be—written points to one large inadequacy in the Freudian project as it is viewed in the late twentieth century. Yet there are notable points of congruity between the Viennese doctor and the Soviet critic. The world of Freudian psychology and Bakhtin's medieval world of carnival laughter both represent, to use the latter's phrase, a "two-world condition" (6). For Bakhtin, this means the simultaneous existence of an official world of church and state, all seriousness, and the unofficial realm of the carnival, full of subversive laughter directed against officialdom in all its forms. For Freud, the two worlds, we might say, are the unconscious world of lust and hostility and the outer world of social conditioning, where those drives are subject to all manner of repressions and sublimations. Freud believes that jokes allow—through the techniques of what he calls wit-work—a safe release of forbidden thoughts and that laughter represents an expression of relief that the energy needed for repression is momentarily unnecessary.[19] For Bakhtin, laughter is a challenge to and circumvention of the authority of the state; for Freud, *the state* is another form of the superego. Such a substitution of one phrase for another is dangerous, of course, and in fact tends to validate an ahistorical view such as Freud's—the different models are only apparently at odds and can be reduced by analogy to the same model.

But there is an important difference between them. What Bakhtin captures that is either missing from or only implicit in Freud's elaborate and very neatly mechanistic model of energy savings and expenditure is just this concept of ambivalence, of the interdependence of life and death and the resulting "incompleteness" of carnivalesque art. And this sense of incompleteness carries over, in Bakhtin's analysis, to the issue of power. As we saw, carnival laughter is not only ambivalent; it is also "universal." Those who laugh are not outside the object of their laughter but included in it and with it. The inseparability of life and death not only inspires ambivalence but also creates a deep union in laughter, the understanding that in laughing at another we must also laugh at ourselves. I think such universality is at work in Sterne and at work in ways that neither Freud nor Hobbes is of much help in understanding, committed as they both are (if in different ways) to a separation of power between those who laugh and those whom they laugh at.

I think that the differences between Hobbes and Freud on the one hand and Sterne and Bakhtin on the other will be clearer if we look at the role of what Freud calls the "second person." As he puts it, "In addition to the one who makes the joke, there must be a second who is taken as the object of the hostile or sexual aggressiveness, and a third in whom the joke's aim of producing pleasure is fulfilled."[20] A nice little triangle: author, audience—and victim. We see here Hobbes's sense that the glory of laughter is gained at someone's expense, yet Freud allows a human connection as well, one we don't see in Hobbes's description, in the shared laughter of joker and listener. True Hobbesian laughter seems to be a two-person event, as when the King of Brobdingnag laughs at Gulliver, and it is the triangulation of Freud's laughter that seems, at first glance, most useful for Sterne. Think, for instance, of "Madam," that high-minded and hypocritical imaginary reader whom Sterne addresses directly from time to time, as in this digression from a discussion of Toby's modesty: "My uncle TOBY SHANDY, Madam, was a gentleman, who, with the virtues which usually constitute the character of a man of honour and rectitude,—possessed one in a very eminent degree, which is seldom or never put into the catalogue; and that was a most extream and unparallel'd modesty of nature; . . . this kind of modesty so possess'd him, and it arose to such a height in him, as almost to equal, if such a thing could be, even the modesty of a woman: That female nicety, Madam, and inward cleanliness of mind and fancy, in your sex, which makes you so much the awe of ours" (48). The sarcastic praise with which he ends his comment clearly identifies poor Madam as the butt of the joke, and Sterne and the rest of his readers can join in a complicitous chortle at her expense. Even more exemplary in this regard is an incident like that involving Phutatorius and the chestnut, when the choleric author of the lewd work "Of Keeping Concubines" is made to suffer quite literally from the overheated groin that seems to have impelled his literary career. In what serves as a jab at Chesterfield's advice, this comic spectacle provokes one witness, Agelastes, whose name means "he who will not laugh," to respond with a "smile" (384). But it is clear that as readers we are meant to follow no such circumspection; our role here is to laugh. This is classic slapstick, whose first rule is always no laughter without a victim.

Such an insistence, however, on a triangular scene of laughter does not coexist comfortably with the traditional portrait of sentimental Sterne, the great celebrator of the powers of sensibility. After all, he is not Oscar Wilde, who commented that it would take someone with a heart of stone not to laugh at the death of Little Nell.[21] Can we reconcile the Sterne of Phutatorius and the burning chestnut with the Sterne who recounts the lachrymose tale of the death of Le Fever? I think Bakhtin's concept of universal laughter provides us with one answer, for that idea frees us from the kind of conceptualization of the role of power in laughter that we see in Hobbes or Freud. Power is clearly not absent from Sterne's laughter, but neither is it the end—the exchange of Walter and Obidiah we looked at before is a good example of the way in which Sterne acknowledges the role of power but also allows some transcendence of it. Let's look further at the pattern of what we might call genital wounding in the novel, for Phutatorius is far from the only victim of that condition.

Phutatorius, like Madam, is a rather unamiable fellow—a paranoid pornographer whose faults are exacerbated by the fact that he hates Yorick, someone whom we instinctively like. But the other most prominent victims of low blows in the book are Uncle Toby and Tristram himself. Toby has been famously wounded in the groin at the siege of Namoor, and Tristram suffers both from forceps and from a falling window. It is difficult to reduce our reaction to any of these wounds to triangulated laughter or to an occasion for us to feel powerful in response to the impotence of another person. The two examples here are rather different, and it is best to look at them individually.

The case of Uncle Toby both is and is not slapstick such as we saw in the scene with Phutatorius. Certainly it is related to slapstick, in that we can feel aggrandized at another's expense. Toby's entirely childlike innocence, gentleness, and modesty are admirable, but they are also in some measure laughable, especially if they are the result of some kind of castration. A grown man and a veteran soldier has been reduced, by a splinter of shrapnel, to a child at play. This is aggressive laughter at its ugliest, but it exists: we can laugh because, quite simply, castration is a deep anxiety, and—this time—it has not happened to us. But origins are always slippery business in *Tristram Shandy*, and Sterne will not easily allow us this safe, better-him-than-me kind of laughter. He denies us this safety because, at least where Toby is concerned, the "groin" becomes a remarkably indefinite place. The widow Wadman is not alone. We all want to know "where" Toby got his wound, she for her purposes and we because we want to know if it *is* his castration we are really laughing at, if it is his final impotence that is the source of his childlike nature. And that, of course, is the knowledge that Toby denies Mrs. Wadman and that Sterne denies us. Thus, in the end we are unable to laugh merely at him but must include ourselves and our own rather horrible desire to fix the location of his wound in some specifiable and disabling place. The power we want to feel—he is wounded, we are complete—is denied us for the simple reason that we never gain secure knowledge of what his wound really is.

When we turn to Tristram, we are faced with what we might call first-person slapstick. The victim is neither an unlikable nor a likable "second person" but our narrator himself. Here again, our laughter at misfortune is tempered by an uncertainty of knowledge, or—to put it better—by a displacement. The forceps destroys Tristram's nose, while the falling window, he strongly hints, merely circumcises him. Yet through innuendo in the first instance ("For by the word *Nose* . . .—I declare, by that word I mean a Nose, and nothing more, or less" [258]) and circumlocution in the second ("thousands suffer by choice, what I did by accident" [449]), we are irresistably led to imagine worse disasters than those we seem to have. The very fact of our uncertainty, however, changes the quality of our laughter. True slapstick depends upon an absolute certainty of knowledge, but what do we do when the man slips on the banana peel offstage? The subject of laughter is shifted, in part, off the victim and back onto our own process of speculation. In short, what Sterne does is to make us laugh simultaneously at genital wounding and at our own desire for genital wounds.

The creation of a universal laughter, one in which power is not polarized, is also reflected in Sterne's creation of his narrator, Tristram Shandy. Writers create narrators for many reasons—to make themselves more or less omniscient, to control information, to explore other voices. Sterne seems to have created Tristram as a way to laugh at himself. Tristram, of course, is not Sterne, in the sense that the events of the novel are not the events of Sterne's life. Yet when Sterne pulls the narrative into the present—as he does, for instance, during the circumcision scene in his reference to the time of writing, "August the 10th, 1761" (449)—the gap between author and narrator temporarily disappears. Hobbes had acknowledged the possibility of self-laughter, noting that the "eminency" we feel may be either at "the infirmity of others" or at "our own formerly." Through the passage of time, he implies, we can treat our past selves as if they were others. Sterne is clearly illustrating the truth of Hobbes's analysis in this regard: by inventing Tristram, he can achieve the distance from his present self that will enable him to laugh. But by the occasional trick of pulling us into the present time of writing, he also keeps that distance from being absolute (the best instance of this technique occurs in volume 7, chapter 38, where Tristram/Sterne admits to being in three different "places" at once). As a result, we have something much closer to a true self-laughter, one not wholly dependent upon the estrangement of self from self that we see in Hobbes.

The genital wounds in *Tristram Shandy* thus cannot be reduced to slapstick, nor can our laughter at them be simplified in Freudian or Hobbesian terms. Our laughter at misfortune in this novel, as in the carnivalesque, always includes ourselves, a universality Sterne enforces by his own self-laughter. Sterne's relation to the materials of his novel—distanced and engaged, powerfully separate yet laughably implicated—becomes the model for our relation to it. John Preston has said that the readers of *Tristram Shandy* must "make up the novel" themselves,[22] meaning that Sterne leaves it to us to reconstruct the pieces of his narrative into a coherent form. Such a reconstruction suggests the power of collaboration in this work: as Preston implies, readers and Sterne "write" it together, and we also laugh our way through it together, not at the expense of a series of "second person" victims but at ourselves, universally.

A comment that Freud makes in a footnote clarifies, I believe, the difference between the kind of limited collaboration his brand of triangulated laughter suggests and the more universal laughter that we find in Sterne. Freud is discussing a subcategory of "nonsense" jokes, jokes he calls in a revealingly bitter formulation "idiocy masquerading as a joke." Such jokes are designed, he says, as a " 'take-in,' and give the person who tells them a certain amount of pleasure in annoying and misleading his hearer."[23] What Freud describes, apparently, is a refinement of Hobbes to a level of active, not merely vicarious, sadism—the joker himself creates the pain that will make him laugh. The discomfort that Freud feels here in the face of this kind of humor is not difficult to account for. If we think of the analytic couch, we can surmise Freud's fears of a patient leading him on with a shaggy-dog tale—a nightmare "interminable analy-sis." The analyst, who is meant to be in the comfortable role of the third person who hears the story, is suddenly thrust unwillingly into the part of the "second person" at whose expense a joke is made. In any event, Freud insists that such take-in humor must be sadistic, and any reader of *Tristram Shandy*, but especially a first-time reader, may feel the anger Freud betrays here. Again, how-ever, I am not sure that such a simple formulation—manipulative Sterne, gullible readership—does justice to our experience of the novel.

The last words of the book certainly acknowledge its status as an exemplary instance of the kind of joke Freud is discussing:

> L——d! said my mother, what is all this story about?—
> A COCK and a BULL, said *Yorick*—And one of the best of its kind, I ever heard. (809)

We have been had here, no doubt. Our tendency as readers to lose ourselves in the events of a fiction is exposed: we thought we were reading about an impotent bull, but the story turns out to be a joking literalization of the metaphor, a cock-and-bull story. What we wanted to take as "real" turned out to be only symbols. More-over, Sterne's decision (if it *was* a decision)[24] to end here is the last joke on our tattered expectations that this novel will in any way represent "The Life and Opinions of Tristram Shandy, Gent." The event in question, like so much of the book, takes place long before our autobiographer was born. He can't begin at the beginning, and he certainly doesn't end at the end. We may remember his com-ment, " '[T]is enough to have thee [the "gentle reader"] in my power" (584). Yet we cannot say that the joke is only on us, that Sterne has achieved a successful take-in, for the author is as big a dupe as we are. At one point, apologizing for yet another digres-sion, he remarks, "[W]hy do I mention it?—Ask my pen,—it gov-erns me,—I govern not it" (500). Tristram is Walter's son, and his plans produce no more controllable results than his father's. What began as "Life and Opinions" ends up as a shaggy-dog story; if he can laugh at our gullibility, we can return a laugh at his inability to follow through, for the take-in is as much his failure as it is our own. Sterne convinces us that he has told a shaggy-dog story on himself as well as on us, and all we can do is laugh together. Both author and audience have been betrayed by desire—for true-sounding fictions, for completeness—and so we conclude as rough equals. And it is on that frustrated plane of equality where we must locate the laughter of this very funny book: we collaborate in the discovery of the frustration that unites us, and we collaborate in the laughter, ambivalent and universal, that results—a laughter that makes us feel good, a true laughter of feeling.

5

The Castle of Otranto:
Political Supernaturalism

The house of fiction has many mansions, none more notable than Horace Walpole's *The Castle of Otranto*—notable in large part because it seems to be that rare thing, an undisputed original. While critics have often argued which was the first novel, no one has ever denied that Walpole originated that extensive branch of the main novelistic line we know as the Gothic novel. For Walpole, who in a preface to the second edition of the book attempted to describe what he thought he had accomplished, his own originality consisted in "reconciling" some features of what he called "ancient" and "modern" romance, thus allowing, he says, free play to "fancy" and "invention" (meaning the supernatural world), while adhering to the "rules of probability" in the delineation of character and motivation (7–8). Apparently, what he wanted to achieve was something like the "natural supernaturalism" that was Coleridge's assigned part, thirty years later, in the *Lyrical Ballads;* as Coleridge described his task in the *Biographia Literaria,* he was to portray supernatural "incidents and agents" but maintain the "dramatic truth . . . as would naturally accompany such situations, supposing them real."[1]

Modern critics of the Gothic novel generally dismiss Walpole's proud claim out of hand. The treatment of character in *Otranto,* far from adhering to any canon of probability, is, they say, wildly implausible and seems far more akin to the abrupt swings in mood and behavior that we associate with Jacobean drama than to the psychological realism of Richardson. In fact, *The Castle of Otranto* remains more often the object of critical scorn than of critical scrutiny,[2] and it is condemned for a host of flaws besides improbable characters, especially uncertainty of tone and a dreadful artificiality of language. In reading the criticism of Walpole, it is difficult to escape the conclusion that originality is the work's only merit and that the only reason it is not a forgotten Gothic novel is that it is the first. But if Walpole's description of what he achieved in his only novel is unsatisfactory, what did he do? What makes *The Castle of Otranto* so original that, despite its manifest flaws, it still merits attention?

Walpole subtitled his work "A Gothic Story," and for all its brevity (it might, more properly, be called a Gothic novella) it manages to encompass whatever understanding of *Gothic* we bring to it. At the time Walpole wrote, *Gothic* often still meant "crude" or "barbarian" (as when Squire Western's "more than Gothic ignorance" is belittled by his sister), and as we have seen, *Otranto* has certainly seemed rough-hewn to many readers. But that was not what Walpole meant by the term, and largely because of his own life-long antiquarian interest and labor, by the mid-eighteenth century the word was beginning to take on the largely aesthetic connotations—medieval and architectural—that it has for us today. Walpole's choice of nomenclature effectively emphasizes the importance of setting in any fiction we call Gothic; indeed, the curious idea of naming a piece of fiction after a house (as opposed to a character or a theme), while not confined to the Gothic tradition, has a long Gothic history that begins with *The Castle of Otranto* and includes such works as *The Mysteries of Udolpho, Northanger Abbey, Wuthering Heights,* and *The House of the Seven Gables.* But though a mysterious house, often in a Continental and Roman Catholic setting, is a common feature of the Gothic novel, it is probably not the defining one. Gothic fiction is also typified by a characteristic emotion—fear—and by the commonest source of that terror—the supernatural. Moreover, there are usually a villainous but strangely charismatic central male figure (the sort of man who later was called the Byronic hero), a threatened maiden, and the possibility of some kind of perverse sexuality, most often incest. Leslie Fiedler has summarized the essence of Gothic fiction in one sharp image: "a maiden in flight."[3] The presence of some of these features is not always enough to earn a novel the label Gothic (*Clarissa,* for instance), nor is the absence of a few enough to disqualify the work from the usual Gothic canon (*Frankenstein,* for example, is considered a Gothic classic, yet it relies on science and technology, not the supernatural, to generate its fear, and the creature in flight therein is a monster, not a maiden). A fiction becomes "Gothic," it seems, when a certain critical mass of these elements is combined. It is not simply a matter of setting or character or subject matter or emotion, nor is it necessary to have all these elements. What is necessary is a sufficiency, which varies from instance to instance.

The Castle of Otranto, fittingly for the original of the breed, does appear to have almost all the possible Gothic characteristics, and its power as generic originator stems, perhaps, from its ability to serve as a kind of dictionary of possibilities from which later artists in the tradition could draw. Indeed, one problem the novel creates for itself is its sheer density: at times, *Otranto* reads like a plot summary of a much longer work, with incident and image crammed together in its pages much as Walpole's own collections crowded the rooms of the miniature Gothic castle he made for himself, Strawberry Hill. Walpole may have found himself attracted to Gothic art because of its insistence on wealth of ornamentation; certainly *Otranto* is as dense with detail as a Gothic screen. In scarcely a hundred pages, we are overwhelmed with thousands of details of plot, character, and setting, any one of which goes on to have a long life in subsequent Gothic fiction: there are the double setting, the castle with its secret passages, and the convent with its secret sexuality; there are both a mysterious prophecy and a curse; there are a tyrant and a maiden, and the threat of incestuous rape; several ghosts walk and speak; crimes are variously committed, uncovered, and revenged; the wind moans, doors creak, the moon casts a flickering light, and something terrifying waits at the top of the stairs; and it all takes place in the forbidden and, to an English audience, provocative Roman Catholic world of medieval Italy.

Walpole certainly had a number of sources to draw on for this Gothic catalog, including the Jacobean drama of the previous century and the "graveyard poetry" of his own day. Burke's influential *A Philosophical Inquiry into the Origins of Our Ideas of the Sublime and Beautiful*, with its analysis of the pleasures of sublime fear, had been published the decade before *The Castle of Otranto*, and Bishop Percy's *Reliques of Ancient English Poetry*, another contemporary work, indicates a revival of interest in medieval ballads, themselves strongly marked by the supernatural and by their ability to provoke a pleasing shiver. There is probably also truth in the supposition, advanced by many, that *Otranto* is a symptom of a reaction against the rationalism in philosophy and decorum in literature that had dominated the first two-thirds of the eighteenth century, an age whose only requirement, Walpole said, was *"cold reason."*[4] Apparently, the sleep of reason did breed monsters—or at least *The Castle of Otranto*.

These familiar suggestions about the origins of an original are useful, but I am not sure they are exhaustive. In particular, the political element, while the subject of some interest, particularly recently,[5] has most generally been downplayed in favor of aesthetic and psychological concerns. The reasons are not far to seek. Although Walpole was a member of Parliament for many years, his political involvements were largely ineffective; on the other hand, even if he had never written *Otranto* he would still be famous as a leading figure in the history of taste. Moreover, he admitted that *Otranto* germinated in a dream of "a castle" and "a gigantic hand in armour" (*Correspondence*, 1: 88). His own biography and commentary have thus tended to shape critical response. The dream information has been particularly appealing to readers of our own time, who have often seen in that origin a license to read the elements of not only *The Castle of Otranto* but Gothic fiction generally as yet more examples of the familiar symbolism of the Freudian unconscious.[6] What is ironic, at least for Walpole, is that such psychological readings ignore one fundamental tenet of psychoanalytic interpretation—suspicion.[7] In his account of the composition of *The Castle of Otranto*, Walpole explicitly disavows any political concern. As he describes his labor, "The work grew on my hands and I grew fond of it—add that I was very glad to think of anything rather than politics" (*Correspondence*, 1: 88). Such an explicit denial normally makes any dream interpreter suspicious, and I think we can usefully ask, What might Walpole be hiding here? In the discussion that follows I want to insist on a strong political emphasis in our understanding of the first Gothic novel. My intent is emphatically not to refute the psychological and especially the sexual approaches to Walpole's work but, rather, to enrich them by exploring the novel's political concerns and obsessions. What I hope we can see is that the political and sexual issues are profoundly implicated in each other. *The Castle of Otranto* does read like a dream, and its images linger in the mind in the same potent way. But the associations behind those images blend the political and the personal in ways that reward careful scrutiny. First, then, I want to explore a train of associations that will connect the dream armor to English political history and to an old but by no means dead idea of a king with two bodies. But those very connections will lead us irresistibly back to personal questions: Horace's father, Robert, was prime minister for twenty years and was arguably the most powerful English politician of the first half of the eighteenth century. As we will see, he has left his imprint on the novel of his youngest son in compelling ways.

The central issue of the novel is legitimacy. In its political form, legitimacy is a question of governance: who rules? But in the context of hereditary monarchy, the question has a sexual meaning as well: how is legitimacy reproduced? When the king dies, who succeeds? *The Castle of Otranto* engages this problem immediately. On the opening page of the story, we learn that Manfred, the prince of Otranto, is anxious to complete the marriage of his only son and heir, Conrad. His anxiety is rooted, it seems, in an "ancient prophecy": "[t]*hat the castle and lordship of Otranto should pass from the present family, whenever the real owner should be grown too large to inhabit it*" (15–16). The inescapable implication is that the "present family" is *not* the "real owner"—that is, the legitimate prince—and that eventually the interests of the rightful monarch will overwhelm, or grow too large for, the line of Manfred. My restatement of the prophecy is, however, far too reasonable, and that phrase *grown too large* harbors a peculiarity not easily rationalized. It would make more sense if the prophecy said that Manfred would be expelled when the legitimate prince was grown *large enough* to inhabit the castle; that would imply some unexceptional process of development—a banished child growing into an avenging adult—that we could understand, and such a model of growth seems in fact to underlie the story of Theodore. But that is not what the prophecy says. And its mysterious and threatening image of gigantism is immediately embodied in the "enormous helmet" (17) that falls from who knows where, crushing Conrad and precipitating the crisis of legitimacy that the novel recounts.

Let us examine the helmet more closely. It is, Walpole tells us, a piece of armor "a hundred times more large than any helmet ever made for [the] human body, and shaded with a proportionate quantity of black feathers." The feathers are given special emphasis as "a mountain of sable plumes" (16–17). The helmet apparently originates in Walpole's dream of "a gigantic hand in armour," and that fragmentary quality of the dream armor is carried over to the story. As we proceed through the novel, we see first this helmet; then, a little later, a "foot and part of a leg," also "clad in armour" (33); then the gigantic saber that Frederic's men carry (62); and finally the huge hand in armor that Bianca spots at the top of the stairs (100). These pieces are not assembled and not seen whole until the novel's apocalyptic conclusion, when the armored form of the long-dead Alfonso, "dilated to an immense magnitude," appears in the middle of the ruined castle (108). But its initial fragmentation and eventual consolidation are not all we know about the armor. In some mysterious way, it is related to the black marble statue of Alfonso that rests on his tomb in the convent a short distance from the castle. When Conrad is killed, the helmet appears to many to resemble the helmet on the statue, and that stone helmet is immediately discovered to be missing. Moreover, when Theodore puts on a suit of armor, Manfred reacts as if Alfonso himself has returned, staring at the young man "with terror and amazement" and crying, "[I]s not that Alfonso?" (80). It is probably worth noting that several characters comment on Theodore's resemblance to a portrait of Alfonso, but Manfred is struck by the similarity only when Theodore puts on armor. Three qualities of the armor, then, stand out initially: it is fragmentary, it is gigantic, and it is somehow connected to the dead prince, Alfonso the Good.

If gigantic and fragmentary armor is both the originating and the dominant image of *The Castle of Otranto*, it is not only an image, a bit of sublime machinery designed to provoke a chill. The armor is also an actor—perhaps the most powerful actor—in the novel's unfolding drama. It is the helmet itself that kills Conrad, but it also does more than kill, and it works for good as well as for vengeance. When Manfred tries to make the helmet into Theodore's prison, that young man discovers a hole it has driven into the courtyard and makes his escape to the convenient secret passage directly below. Moreover, the sable plumes wave ominously whenever Manfred's plans become especially criminal (see 23, 56). We could multiply such examples of the armor's direct agency in the story, culminating in the destruction of the corrupted castle by the now-reassembled armor at the novel's climax.

Walpole's use of the armor can be seen as an example of what we might call, playing off Coleridge, political supernaturalism. The supernatural component may seem obvious enough—the restless ghost of the murdered Alfonso, a kind of vengeful puppet master, uses his own fragmented and transformed armor as an agent of revenge against an illegitimate ruler. But I think the situation is more complicated. I would suggest that a relationship exists between the armor in the novel and certain traditions of royal and state funerals, particularly those involving effigies. The symbolism of those occasions seems both to have exerted a powerful influence on the creation of *The Castle of Otranto* and to mark the implications this novel has for the issue of political legitimacy.

Effigies first appeared in English royal funeral ceremonies in the thirteenth century, at the burial of Edward II, and they spread to France about a century later. The precise reasons for their initial appearance are uncertain (and probably practical, having to do with the competing demands of politics, whose requirements for pomp necessitated the delay of burial, and nature, which insists on promptitude in such matters).[8] What is clear is that over the next few centuries, rituals of elaborate significance were developed. We should note that the use of effigies evolved differently in England and France, French customs being more detailed and more consistent (here, too, they order these matters better in France). But in both countries, the use of royal funeral effigies became an opportunity for a public staging of the political doctrine of an undying kingship, the doctrine known in England as "the king's two bodies." That doctrine, summarized briefly, grew by analogy out of theological speculations about a dual-natured Christ, and it contended that the monarch had his own dual existence, as a mortal man encased in a "body natural" and as an immortal and corporate king, the "body politic." Kings die, but the kingship never does. In terms of the issue at the heart of *Otranto*, the body politic is what legitimizes the succession of bodies natural; it is the unique principle of legitimacy that survives throughout the generations of a dynasty and unites them.

The great scholar of this idea, Ernst Kantorowicz, argues that the normal order of things—a visible body natural, an invisible body politic—is significantly reversed in the funeral ritual of the royal effigy: the dead body natural is invisible in its coffin, while the normally intangible body politic is, for once, visibly present on top of the coffin in the form of the effigy.[9] In other words, at the time of the monarch's death, the ghostly body politic is given a real, if temporary, form. The point is tricky, however. Part of the power of dynastic succession is the way it avoids the problem of an interregnum, and the doctrine of the king's two bodies would have little force did it not insist that the body politic *instantaneously* occupies the body natural of the legitimate successor at the moment of the old king's death. The problem is that there is an intrinsic liminal danger in any moment of political transition, and what Kantorowicz's analysis reminds us is that the symbolism of the effigy, the rendering temporarily visible of the body politic, responds to an emotional need to see what is actually being transferred from one natural body to the next, even if that transfer has already occurred. The effigy, that is, serves as a reminder of the immortality principle inherent in a belief in a two-bodied king, making outward and visible a spiritual truth at precisely the moment when its reality needs most strongly to be asserted. To put it another way, the problem that the effigy mediates is that of separation. Doctrinally, there is no transition between rulers, and the separation and reincorporation of the body politic occurs simultaneously; however, psychologically and emotionally, the populace must experience the transition, and the funeral effigy helps make that necessary process possible.[10]

The sexual implications of the doctrine are worth pausing over. On the one hand, the idea of the body politic implies a transcendence of generation—because it is immortal, it does not need to reproduce. After all, the kingship never dies. But because kings stubbornly persist in dying, the body politic also requires legitimate reproduction; without a succession of bodies natural, it has no place to go. A dynasty, therefore, suggests both an escape from reproduction, in that its legitimizing principle is unchanging and immortal, and an extraordinary reproductive imperative, since the body politic must always have someplace to call home. The body politic (and by extension, the effigy that represents it) thus has an oddly ambivalent sexuality: it is both beyond sex and deeply sexualized, both immortal in itself and absolutely dependent upon human reproduction. Because of that dependence, we could say that the body politic authorizes the sexuality of the monarch.

The use of effigies at the funerals of English monarchs was at its peak in the sixteenth and seventeenth centuries, and the practice fell into decline after the Restoration. Later royal funerals became more private affairs, elaborate still but without the vast symbolic staging (and cost!) of these traditional burials.[11] It is, of course, impossible not to see a connection between such a shift in English royal funeral practice and the profound political crises of the seventeenth century. The institution of a constitutional monarchy with the Glorious Revolution of 1688 by no means marked the end of the doctrine of the king's two bodies (as we will see, that doctrine retained full legal force), but the new climate, given especially the renewed institutional anti-Catholicism, was not a happy one for political supernaturalism. Effigies—those temporary embodiments, icons if you will, of a spiritual truth—made no appearance at the funerals of the Hanoverian monarchs.

What, then, do defunct funeral practices and the political theology (the phrase is Kantorowicz's) they supported have to do with *The Castle of Otranto?* The significant connection, as I have already hinted, is the armor of Alfonso, and I think that Walpole's novel begins to make more sense if we view that armor as importantly related to the kind of funeral effigy just discussed. As at a royal funeral, a normally invisible body politic has become quite visible, but here in new and frightening ways.

We must return to the death-dealing helmet that we began with. As we saw, that monstrous casque turns out to be a magnified and transported version of the helmet that adorns the tomb of Alfonso in the convent a short distance from the castle. While Walpole nowhere describes the exact appearance of this statue, we can reasonably imagine it to look like any one of thousands of such tombs throughout England and the Continent: a reclining figure in armor resting on the sarcophagus of the dead man. Such statues are not the same thing, of course, as those effigies which figured in royal funerals, but a clearly analogous relationship exists. Both statue and effigy rest visibly on top of a hidden body; both represent something unchanging and incorruptible in distinction to the interior decay we know about but cannot see. Such an analogy is further licensed in the case of the statue of Alfonso, since he was not merely a knight or other noble but the monarch of Otranto. If we project English doctrine back onto the medieval Italy that Walpole imagined—and I believe we must—Alfonso is someone who possessed both a human body and served as the host of the undying kingship of his principality. The connection of statue and effigy is further enforced by the detail Walpole emphasizes so strongly, that of the black feathers on the casque. Such "sable plumes" would have been a typical part of funeral pageantry.

The best indication, however, that the armor of Alfonso should be seen to function like a funeral effigy is the way we can view it as a very particular kind of ghost—the body politic. As we have seen, the effigy serves to make visible the undying kingship at the perilous moment of its transfer to a new body natural. But as we learn in the last, packed pages of *The Castle of Otranto*, the principality did not pass from Alfonso to a legitimate heir (that "real owner" of the prophecy); it passed to Ricardo, Manfred's grandfather, who poisoned his prince and usurped the throne. My premise, then, is that the mortuary monument on Alfonso's tomb, that effigylike statue, acts in the novel as the avenging ghost of the body politic, and that the power that thwarts Manfred is not the spirit of Alfonso as an individual but rather the undying kingship of Otranto. Walpole's decision to make the armor the most powerful actor in the novel is, we might say, the literalization of a literalization. If the funeral effigy is a spiritual reality made temporarily visible, then the "clank of more than mortal armor" (108) that resounds through this tale represents an attempt to make that spiritual reality not only visible but animate, a kind of armorial transsubstantiation. The strong air of the supernatural inherent in a custom like a funeral effigy is here pushed, by a logic of reification, to a new level, but it is still part of the same logic that created the ceremony of the effigy in the first place. In France, in the days before the king's body was actually committed to the grave, his effigy had elaborate meals prepared for its consumption.[12] In its own way, *The Castle of Otranto* seems to ask, What if one day that effigy should actually sit up and *eat*? If the symbol is true, who are we to set limits on its power?

One way to make clearer what Walpole has done is to think about his story in relation to one of the sources and inspirations that the novelist acknowledged, *Hamlet*. In C. S. Lewis's remarkably evocative list of the elements of that tragedy—"night, ghosts, a castle, a lobby where a man can walk four hours together, a willow-fringed brook and a sad lady drowned, a graveyard and a terrible cliff above the sea"[13]—we can discern how *Hamlet* itself went a long way toward establishing the code of Gothic conventions. We could even go so far as to say that had Shakespeare rewritten his play with a different central character and called his tragedy *Claudius*, we would have something very close (in plot, anyway) to *The Castle of Otranto*. But for all their similarities, there is one striking difference between Gothic drama and Gothic novel. The spirit of old Hamlet is indeed arrayed in the armor in which he once smote the sledded Polacks, but he remains always the rather impotent ghost of an individual, a figure of moral force but no physical power of his own, one who begs for remembrance and for a revenge he himself is helpless to execute. In *Otranto*, however, as we have seen, the armor *is* the agent, and the effigy, no longer a

mere symbol of an abstraction, takes upon itself the task of revenge. *Otranto*'s Hamlet-figure, Theodore, may prove his worth
and valor in the course of the novel, but it is no part of his task to
set the time right. The ghostly armor does justice for itself.

The Castle of Otranto, much more than *Hamlet*, is obsessed with
dynastic concerns, and the justice that governs the outcome of the
novel is interested far more in reestablishing the correct line of
inheritance than in gaining vengeance for the sufferings of Alfonso
the individual. The work of the giant armor is less to punish Manfred (though that occurs) than to end his line, the false dynasty
established at the time of Ricardo's usurpation. In short, what Manfred wants is to reproduce his line, and what the ghostly body
politic of Alfonso's dynasty wants is to stop him. As we learn on
the penultimate page of the novel, the usurping line represented
by Manfred will retain power as long as there is "issue-male from
Ricardo's loins . . . to enjoy it" (109), and it is that line which the
armor destroys. The battle in this novel, then, is not between a live
man, Manfred, and a dead one, Alfonso; it is between competing
dynasties, only one of which has the true immortality principle and
guarantor of legitimacy, the body politic, on its side.

To underline the intermingling of the sexual and political here,
Manfred's attempts at reproduction are explicitly criminal. In his
attempts to compel his wife to divorce him and in his simultaneous
efforts to force himself on his dead son's betrothed, Isabella (a siege
that amounts to the threat of incestuous rape), Manfred's sexuality
is revealed to be as illegitimate as his claim to the throne. His roles
as a political and a sexual criminal become synonymous. Literally,
he has no right to do what he does. Alfonso, on the other hand,
has reproduced legitimately: he had a daughter who, in turn, bore
a son, Theodore. Unlike Manfred's, Alfonso's line has never failed,
even during the long years of estrangement from its rightful authorizing principle, the body politic.

There is a troubling question here: why does the body politic
wait three generations before it restores the legitimate dynastic
line? Later, I will suggest one, possibly seditious interpretation, but
another is offered by the effigy itself. When Manfred announces
the dual wedding—himself to Isabella, Frederic's daughter, and his
own daughter, Matilda, to Frederic—in the presence of the statue
of Alfonso, three drops of blood fall from its nose. Jerome immediately announces, "Behold! . . . [M]ark this miraculous indication

that the blood of Alfonso will never mix with that of Manfred!" (93). Frederic, we know, is "nearest in blood" (57) to Alfonso, though he is not in the direct line of succession, and the armor had begun its bloody work in order to prevent his daughter's marriage to Conrad, just as it now bleeds to learn of the double marriage of fathers and daughters from the competing lines. Clearly, the effigy comes to life in order to prevent the pseudolegitimacy created by a marriage between Manfred's clan and anyone who has a tincture of Alfonso's blood. The image of a statue with a nosebleed is, of course, comic, but it does at least hint at castration, at the halting of Alfonso's bloodline. As such, it is a reminder of the tacit sexuality of all such effigies. At the end of the novel, the marriage we finally get, that of Theodore and Isabella, will unite the blood of Alfonso in both its direct and a collateral line, a quasi-incestuous coupling that announces the restoration of the pure and legitimate line. We can think here of the pharaohs, who also married incestuously in order to maintain the purity of their dynasties.

To summarize, then, the revenge of the effigy is directed not against Manfred personally or against the original usurper, Ricardo, but against the line they both represent. Because that line is politically illegitimate, it is Manfred's children, Conrad and Matilda, who must die. Manfred, for all his bluster and threat, is not wholly bad (see 30, 35, 55), and he turns criminal only in defense of a dynasty that he did not establish but feels compelled to continue. As if to emphasize this point, Manfred does not, as we might expect, die at the novel's end but is allowed to take on "the habit of religion" (110). The effect is to direct the novel's treatment of the issue of legitimacy and justice away from the behavior of individuals and onto political abstractions. It is the *idea* of legitimacy—in the tangible form of armor at once ghostly and gigantic—that ultimately corrects the social order, for every human actor in the story is helpless to effect events. For the three-day time span of the novel, the body politic is in charge; what it wants is a legitimate succession to Alfonso (which is to say, a legitimate line of bodies natural), and that legitimacy is what it finally achieves. It is then that the ghost can disappear, for the body politic at long last has a "rightful" home in Theodore, grown large enough now to take his throne. Here, too, we can see the logic behind the armor's fragmentation and reassembly. As fragments, the armor suggests the incompleteness of a body politic without a legitimate human body to call home; it is the state that is fragmented under such conditions. The moment when the armor is put back together again is the moment when the state itself is again whole.

There is, it seems, a view of the self, of identity, implicit in all this. It is, after all, a suit of armor—not an individual or the ghost of an individual—that does the necessary business of setting Otranto right again. Put another way, we might say that the legitimacy of Alfonso's line is not only represented but maintained by a hollowed-out remnant—a literally empty effigy that is more powerful than any character in the novel. We could follow this idea to some rather banal conclusion about the political superiority of laws to people, but I am more interested in the representational implications. Eve Kosofsky Sedgwick has suggested that Gothic fiction is generally concerned with surfaces at least as much as with depths, and that it displays a significant, rather than incompetent, disregard for the creation of "rounded" characters—the Gothic, that is, is habitually intrigued with flat representations.[14] In *Otranto*, this phenomenon takes the form of the defeat of personality by impersonality, of the frantic and contradictory individual, Manfred, by an effigy representing the impersonal immortality principle of a dynastic line. For the dynasty, individuals are themselves only hollow receptacles whose selfhood is constituted by a legitimacy that is, in the end, only passing through.

Two questions arise at this point. What evidence is there that Walpole knew about these doctrines and the customs that accompanied them? And what is a deist and the staunchly Whig son of Robert Walpole doing writing a novel in which the operative political ideology is strongly tinted with a belief in a quasi-divine kingship? As noted earlier, the doctrine of the king's two bodies, while symbolically and probably theologically not to the taste of post-1688 England, retained full legal force. Blackstone's monumental *Commentaries*, which were first published in 1765, the year after *Otranto*, include a long and eloquent exposition of the idea of a two-bodied king, in language that goes back to the inception of the doctrine: "for . . . when we say the demise of the crown, we mean only that in consequence of the disunion of the king's natural body from his body politic, the kingdom is transferred or demised to his successor; and so the royal dignity remains perpetual." And, "The king never dies. . . . For immediately upon the decease of the reigning prince in his natural capacity, his kingship or imperial dignity . . . without any interregnum or interval, is vested at once in his heir."[15] That is, if the spectacular dramaturgy of the royal funeral effigy had disappeared, the doctrine that created that bit of theater had not. Moreover, in Westminster Abbey, actual effigies (which is to say, the figures carried in the processional) of long-dead monarchs were still on display, and Walpole comments on them in his letters (*Correspondence*, 9:373–74). Obviously, too, there was plenty of Gothic tomb statuary that Walpole would have seen. Given Walpole's extraordinary and permanently influential interest in the medieval world and in Gothic art, then, it would be surprising if he did not know a good deal about the meaning of effigies and the conduct of a royal funeral for a two-bodied king.

There is more, and things here become complicated in terms of Walpole's own beliefs, allegiances, and family history. While it is true that public royal funerals complete with effigy went out of fashion before the eighteenth century, grand state funerals, particularly for national heroes, did not.[16] Perhaps the most spectacular funeral of the century took place on 9 August 1722, when John Churchill, Duke of Marlborough, was laid to rest after almost eight weeks of preparations (he had died in mid-June). Among the thousands of Londoners watching the solemn ceremony was five-year-old Horace Walpole, and before we discount the effect of the funeral on such a young child, we should attend to his own comment more than sixty years later: "[N]o, all this cannot have happened in one life!" he wrote in 1785. "I have seen a mistress of James II, the Duke of Marlborough's burial, three or four wars, the whole career, victories and death of Lord Chatham, the loss of America, the second conflagration of London" (*Correspondence*, 25:558–59). It is clear that Walpole, near seventy, considered this funeral one of the great events of his life. But what does a general's funeral, however grand, have to do with *The Castle of Otranto* and the avenging armor of Alfonso the Good?

I would suggest that the funeral of the old duke provided Walpole with a set of images that he could draw on in composing *Otranto*. Those images, I hope to show, were appealing, in part anyway, because of the way in which they resonated with the ideas of funeral effigies and two-bodied kings already considered. But that resonance is itself problematic. What we have are images that are easily conflated, but the ideas suggested by those images are not so happily reconciled.

My knowledge of Marlborough's funeral is based on the wonderful account provided by James Sutherland, which in turn draws on contemporary newspaper stories. Several points in his narrative of the event are relevant here. One is his detailed summary of the procession itself, complete with trumpeters, kettledrums, banner carriers, heralds, no less than seven riderless horses (all draped in black, some with black feathers and plumes), and so on. There were more than 250 persons with specifically assigned roles in the procession—and that number does not take into account the thousands of soldiers (both foot and horse), including ten generals, who preceded and followed this already-impressive train. Any reader of *The Castle of Otranto* is immediately reminded of the similar procession in the novel when Frederic and his troops arrive. That is not a funeral, but it is certainly funeral*like*, with its "led horse" (61), and the hundred knights struggling like pallbearers to carry the weight of the enormous sword they bring with them. More significant for our purposes, however, is the centerpiece of Marlborough's procession. There, Sutherland tells us, rode "a magnificent funeral chariot . . . surmounted by waving plumes and trophies of war." On top of the chariot "the coffin lay on a great bed of state for all to see," and on that coffin rested "a complete suit of armour, with a general's truncheon clasped in the right hand, . . . and a rich sword in a scabbard of crimson velvet buckled to the side."[17]

The image of Marlborough's funeral armor connects to *The Castle of Otranto* in several ways. First, it seems related to all the Gothic tomb statuary that represents an armorial figure at rest on a coffinlike base; as such, it is a kind of model for the tomb of Alfonso in particular. Second, the armor at Marlborough's funeral functions much like a royal funeral effigy, in that it is an image of permanence covering an invisible but all too well known decay, an image, moreover, that is the very focal point of the entire ceremony. As at a royal funeral, two bodies—one magnificent and whole, one hidden and rotting—are at the center of a grand spectacle designed to celebrate at once continuity and change. Marlborough was no king, but his splendid suit of armor certainly works to imply a sempiternal English military glory. From his earliest years, then, Walpole had an unforgettable picture in his mind of a kind of power that death cannot destroy. It is also worth remembering that Alfonso's armor is, above all, gigantic, and of course all armor appears gigantic when one is five years old.

But if we remember his biography, Walpole's associations with the funeral must have run far more deeply than this. Marlborough's funeral was overtly meant to celebrate the immortal heroic achievement of the victor of Blenheim, but it also, tacitly but unmistakably, announced the power of young Horace's father, the "Great Man" himself, Robert Walpole. According to Sutherland, the extravagance of Marlborough's funeral was not simply a spontaneous outpouring of national grief; more accurately, it was a carefully staged piece of Whig theater, designed to throw in the faces of the opposition Tories the shameful fact of their removal, a decade before, of Marlborough from his office as commander in chief at the time of the Peace of Utrecht. Every banner, every kettledrum, every horse with an empty saddle and waving black plumes represented a none-too-subtle dig at those who had removed so manifest an example of military greatness from his command. But the ceremony was more than an elaborate form of factional spite. The funeral occurred precisely in the middle of Robert Walpole's successful attempt to consolidate his own political supremacy. His chief rival, Sunderland, had died in April, and two months after the funeral, he would persuade Parliament to suspend habeas corpus in response to his largely manufactured claims of renewed Jacobite conspiracy. Indeed, Atterbury—dean of Westminster, presiding clergy at the funeral, and Jacobite fellow traveler—was arrested a scant two weeks later and packed off, first to the Tower and then into exile. The elder Walpole, who had seen his political ups and downs in the previous decade, was thus at this moment pulling irrevocably into his hands the power he would hold for another twenty years,[18] and his youngest son, in watching this impressive display, was in a real sense watching his own father's power on display. Like the rest of London, young Horace saw a memorable bit of political theater; unlike the rest, though, he was the director's son.

Clearly that dream image of a "gigantic hand in armor" which originates *The Castle of Otranto* is a profoundly overdetermined symbol. Walpole called it "a very natural dream for a head filled like mine with Gothic story" (*Correspondence*, 1:88), but far more than Gothic story lies behind that armed vision. We can identify a number of associations: Gothic tomb statuary, royal effigies, the idea of a two-bodied king, the funeral of a general, the power of a father. And these associations are by no means consistent, for the armor of

Alfonso points both to the new political order in England and to the order that passed away in 1688. On the one hand, Walpole's dream is a recollection of Marlborough's funeral armor, which was meant to be a kind of effigy of Whig legitimacy, an assertion of the vitality of the Whigs' own body politic. As such, that armor affirmed the justice of the Glorious Revolution and the limited constitutional monarchy it instituted. On the other hand, however, Marlborough's armor was a dangerous symbol, for it was co-opted from the prerevolutionary ideology it was meant to deny. That is, insofar as it conjured up images from the past, those images were connected not to a limited and Hanoverian monarchy but to a more absolutist Stuart line, infected with Catholics and dangerous notions of a semidivine kingship.

If we turn from the funeral to the novel, what we see is that Alfonso's armor also wants to affirm legitimacy, but, like Marlborough's effigy, it seems a bit equivocal about what kind of legitimacy it wants to announce. The political equivocation in the novel may be clearer if we look more closely at the role of the usurper, Manfred. We are immediately presented with a problem: at first glance, it is allegorically easy to identify Manfred with James II, the king (in the words of Blackstone) whose "misconduct . . . amounted to an *endeavour* to subvert the constitution" (83, his emphasis). Manfred and James both, by the impropriety of their actions, lose the name of king and thus, in a legal sense, desert their office. Blackstone insists that James was not removed from the throne but abdicated it, and we can view Manfred's crimes—his pursuit of Isabella, his murder of Matilda—as the mark of his own abdication. But if the novel validates such an identification of Manfred with the last Stuart king, it also powerfully resists it.

Blackstone's comments on the revolution of 1688 make it clear, in legal and constitutional terms (as opposed to the sentimental ones we derive from Walter Scott), the source of Jacobite appeal. The decision in 1688 to vacate the throne was a unique event in British political history. If the doctrine of a two-bodied king was designed, in part, to eliminate the problem of an interregnum, then on this one occasion an interregnum occurred, and did so in terms of not Cromwell's republic (Charles II was alive) but in the body politic itself. As Blackstone puts it, at that time "there was no king in being" (81). In other words, for the first and only time in English history, the king had only one body, the ghostly body politic, and it temporarily had no place to go: "the kingly office remain[ed], though King James was no longer king" (83). The wisdom of Parliament eventually relocated the office in William and Mary and then in the Hanovers, and as we have seen, eighty years later Blackstone can assert, with apparently perfect confidence, that the king never dies and that an interregnum is impossible. But the one exception remained, like a scar on the national memory, and for sixty years after (indeed, much longer, if we think of a figure like Scott), the Jacobites could always strike a powerful chord in some by saying that James and his heirs were the legitimate line and that the decision by Parliament to vacate the throne was wrong, was an act of usurpation. In this light, it is as easy to see Manfred as King George as it is to see him as King James. We should recall that George III—the third Hanover king, that is—had taken the throne just four years before *Otranto* appeared. Manfred is also the heir to a throne established by his grandfather. The stated moral of the tale, *"that the sins of the fathers are visited on the children to the third and fourth generation"* (5), is a potentially seditious one in eighteenth-century England. *The Castle of Otranto*, from this viewpoint, asks the allegorical question, What if the body politic did not enter the Hanover line, just as it refused to enter the line of Manfred? Lending credence to this line of thought is the fact that *Otranto* consistently validates the legitimacy of the exile (and exile, of course, is one primary Jacobite reality). Alfonso dies while abroad, and Theodore has only just returned after years of foreign imprisonment. Indeed, it is his return from exile, along with the proposed marriage of Conrad, that seems to bestir the body politic from three generations of sleep.

I do not want to suggest that Walpole's novel should be read as a veiled Jacobite allegory. What interests me is that Alfonso's armor can be read politically in two ways at once: as both an image of the immortality of kingship and of the necessity and justice of removing bad kings. In English history, those ideas are meant to coexist (as we see in an authority like Blackstone), but they do not coexist peacefully: witness, from those who deny the legitimacy of the Glorious Revolution, more than a half-century of Jacobite threats, conspiracies, and actual invasions and, from the extremest supporters of the Protestant succession, the eighteenth-century equivalent of red-baiting, complete with trumped-up charges, inflated claims, and scare tactics, the political arts of which Robert Walpole was the

master. It is hard to escape here a sense that the political ambivalence we see in *The Castle of Otranto* mirrors the kind of oedipal
ambivalence sons normally feel for fathers. Marlborough's funeral
armor may have transmuted itself into Alfonso's gigantic armor
because it could symbolize, for Walpole, both his father's invincible
strength and authority—political and sexual—and, at the same
time, a divinely sanctioned alternative, something permanent and
pure and totally impatient with the politics of money and alliance
and intrigue with which Robert Walpole is so often associated[19] and
for which Manfred's behavior in the novel can serve as a partial
representation. The younger Walpole's own sense of political failure is well known, and his insistence that, in writing the novel, he
was thinking of "anything rather than politics" may reflect his
inability to practice the kind of politics his father mastered. If Marlborough's armor served as an image of the authorizing power behind Horace Walpole's father, that particular body politic had not
passed to Horace.

In *Otranto*, armor successfully suggests both the father's power
(in that Alfonso restores justice and legitimately reproduces his
line) and a wish for paternal powerlessness (in the reiterated pic-
tures of Manfred's essential impotence). That is, "the gigantic hand
in armor" is the hand of the good father, but it is also the hand that
will punish the hated father. And that doubleness is mirrored by
the fate of the novel's two sons, Conrad and Theodore, one of
whom is crushed and one of whom is crowned, thus both damning
and ensuring the son's guilty wish. Impossible, yes, but then
dreams promise not plausibility but wish fulfillment.[20]

Yet such ambivalence and such an impossible resolution of it,
while clearly carrying a strong personal charge, equally clearly
have larger implications. To reduce the remarkable divisions of *The
Castle of Otranto* to oedipal rage and guilt is not inaccurate, but it
fails to do justice to the full significance of the first Gothic novel. In
part because of his own unique family history, Walpole's private
emotions constantly work as powerful analogies to national feelings, to problems and questions that the English people were still
laboring to forget. Blackstone—to return to that spokesman one
last time—explicitly calls on the nation to repress and to forget the
troubling decisions of 1688: "But care must be taken not to carry
this inquiry farther, than merely for instruction and amusement.
The idea, that the consciences of posterity were concerned in the

rectitude of their ancestors' decisions, gave birth to those dangerous heresies, which so long disturbed the state, but at length are all
happily extinguished. . . . Whereas, our ancestors having most in-
disputably a competent jurisdiction to decide this great and important question, and having in fact decided it, it is now become our
duty at this distance of time to acquiesce in their determination"
(82). It is perhaps the oldest argument in any apologist's arsenal—
what is done is done. The example of *The Castle of Otranto*, however, suggests that in the national unconscious, no more than in
the personal one, nothing is ever over, no old feelings, apparently
buried, ever and completely "happily extinguished." This novel,
meant as an escape from politics and designed to serve the safe
dulce et utile of Blackstone's "instruction and amusement," calls up
again the old nagging questions about legitimacy and the nature of
kingship, the old fears about usurpation and revenge.

What we see, then, in this, the first Gothic novel, is a political
return of the repressed. All those elements in English politics
thought by the eighteenth century to be so dangerous and apparently so safely dead by the time Walpole wrote—the potent mixture
I have called political supernaturalism—appear again here in the
displaced but still-readable sign of a gigantic hand in armor. Of
course, we can take this "return" cynically. We might say that Walpole recognized that, whatever its other merits, the constitutional
monarchy of Georgian England did not make for very good Gothic
novels. But despite the clear evidence of Walpole's ability to shape
public taste, I think that the armor of Alfonso carries more interesting emotional and political implications. *The Castle of Otranto* is a
flawed novel in many ways, but we should not ignore its ability to
conjure up the ghosts of both family life and English politics. As
the history of the genre unfolds, the power of Gothic fiction often
resides in its ability to find a tangible form for intangible realities,
most especially the terror that lurks on the other side of family
harmony. But in his one novel, Horace Walpole found a way to give
form not just to what is psychologically frightening in personal and
family life but to what was politically troubling in English history.

6

Emma:
The New Courtship

Like most love stories, Jane Austen's *Emma* revolves around two primary questions: suitability and difficulty. The first question concerns who belongs together and why; the second examines what keeps such couples apart. The questions may seem to contradict each other, but in fact they work intimately together. Erotic narratives, novels included, generally labor first to create desire by bringing suitable couples into proximity and then to sustain that desire by finding plausible reasons to delay their union. In short, what we demand in a love story is an attraction and an obstacle, and these two fundamental principles of construction may be honored in a variety of ways. *Emma* is typical of works of genius in that it manages fully to embody this very old tradition even while it contrives to rewrite its possibilities. Austen's novel represents both a paradigm and a revolution, an achievement that rests significantly on the role obstacles play in the story. Since *Emma* ends with three weddings, the first question we have to ask is, What took them so long?

That question is of particular moment in *Emma* because of the way the novel opens. The three couples who marry at the end of the book are essentially already together at the beginning. Harriet Smith has "just returned from a long visit in the country" (23), where her beauty has won the heart of Robert Martin, whose own good qualities, in turn, have made a favorable impression on her. Frank Churchill and Jane Fairfax, we eventually learn, become engaged at about the time the novel opens (i.e., October—see 7 and 395). And the very first chapter of *Emma* recounts how Knightley, who has just ridden the sixteen-mile journey from London, promptly walks a mile in the dark to pay a courtesy call on Emma and her father. Knightley is so attentive to his neighborly duties that it is easy for us to follow the Woodhouses' lead and take such a visit for granted, but the fact remains that the household scene we observe as the curtain rises on the action—Emma and Knightley conversing, Mr. Woodhouse complaining, all within the confines of Hartfield—is the same one we imagine as the curtain falls four hundred pages later. Thus three suitable couples are already in proximity when the novel begins, and the challenge that Austen sets for herself as an artist is how believably she may delay their three weddings.

To appreciate Austen's achievement here, I want to pause and consider in some detail the history and purpose of obstacles in love stories. I have suggested that obstacles are connected to desire, and two comments, one by Plato and the other by Freud, help clarify that connection. In the *Symposium,* Socrates insists that "everyone . . . who feels desire, desires what is not in his present power of possession, and desire and love have for their objects things or qualities which a man does not at present possess but which he lacks."[1] Necessarily, then, desire is predicated upon an absence, and obstacles thus function to create or serve as an image of the absence that defines desire. Freud reminds us, in a comment that says at least as much about why we read love stories as about how we ruin our lives, that we actually seek out (either actively or unconsciously) such obstacles: "It can easily be shown that the physical value of erotic needs is reduced as soon as their satisfaction becomes easy. An obstacle is required in order to heighten libido; and where natural resistances to satisfaction have not been sufficient, men have at all times erected conventional ones so as to be able to enjoy love."[2] In erotic narratives, obstacles serve both a psychological and an aesthetic purpose. They remind us that obstacles are the origin of desire, and they also mimetically re-create or represent that state of longing. Obstacles make desire *visible,* and they work to achieve for readers of such stories an image of what is, after all, a negative state.

The list of obstacles available to writers of love stories is both long and familiar. One convenient summary is provided by Milton's Adam, who appears to recognize that after the fall, all romance will turn on a question of frustration:

> . . . for either
> He never shall found out fit mate, but such
> As some misfortune brings him, or mistake,
> Or whom he wishes most shall seldom gain
> Through her perverseness, but shall see her gained
> By a far worse, or if she love, withheld

By parents, or his happiest choice too late
Shall meet, already linked and wedlock-bound
To a fell adversary, his hate or shame:
Which infinite calamity shall cause
To human life, and household peace confound.

(book 10, l. 898–908)

Of course, what might be "infinite calamity" in real life is precisely what we seek in narratives of all kinds, but Adam's catalog here is an inclusive list of obstacles for not only tragic love stories (we can discern here, for example, the lineaments of *Romeo and Juliet*, Tristan and Iseult, and *Anna Karenina*) but comic ones as well. If we remove from the passage its grim misogyny and bleak predictions (Milton here, with the epic poet's privilege, is doubtless projecting his own domestic miseries onto human history), what is left is simply a list of all those difficulties, one of which every such story requires: disapproving parents, unrequited love, an obviously inferior rival, a previous commitment, poor judgment, plain bad luck. All these problems have tragic potential, certainly, but they are also necessary ingredients in any recipe for a happy ending. The difference between comic love stories and tragic ones is whether suitability triumphs over difficulty or difficulty dooms suitability—in both kinds of narrative, however, difficulty must be present.

Another important distinction needs to be made between what we might call external versus internal obstacles. By *external obstacles*, I mean difficulties that lie outside the hearts and minds of the lovers. Such problems tend to be subsumed by Adam's word *misfortune*, and include the various kinds of blocking characters he describes. Love stories based on the bad luck of an external difficulty resolve themselves into two classic plots: adultery and family opposition. In the former, the obstacle is a rival, and I would suggest that whenever a rival exists, the story has an adulterous feel, whether or not anyone is married.[3] In the latter plot, the problem is the family of one or both lovers; such opposition, because it represents family intervention in the sexual life of the child, gives such plots an incestuous tone. These two plots can be interwoven, for the family can serve quite well in the role of the rival. We can think here of *Clarissa*, where the Harlowes not only oppose Lovelace but impose Solmes, leaving Clarissa with an ugly choice between adultery and incest. In the broadest sense, love stories with an external obstacle center on problems of what anthropology calls exogamy—literally, "marriage out," but the word suggests any sexual alliance that cuts across group lines. In such stories, a lover's allegiance to some group (at the most basic level, the family, but also a class, religion, nation, or race) is threatened by an attractive outsider, and the difficulty thus becomes a painful choice between the promptings of the heart and an externalized loyalty to the group. Will Juliet, for example, love and marry against the wishes of the Capulets? That the Capulets and Montagues have chosen to define themselves as opposing groups with no apparent good reason underlines our sense that group classifications are arbitrary, but they are also inescapable, and the inescapability of such distinctions returns us to the idea that external difficulties belong to a world of "misfortune."

Adam rhetorically opposes *misfortune* to *mistake,* and the concept of the mistake usually governs those love stories in which the obstacle is internal. In these narratives, the obstacle is located precisely within the hearts and minds of one or both lovers. While the kinds of mistakes such lovers may make are legion, plots with an internal obstacle can again be conveniently divided into two sorts, both of them focused specifically on problems of knowledge: mistakes about one's own feelings and mistakes about the other's feelings. Still, all stories with an internal obstacle seem based on the same premise. To paraphrase Henry James, it is very hard to know any human heart, even one's own.[4] And so, as we read Pamela's breathless letters, we observe a problem of self-knowledge, since we are well aware long before she is that she is really in love with Mr. B.; and, in *Pride and Prejudice,* we watch Elizabeth Bennet's smug ignorance of the true state of Darcy's affections, a problem of knowledge about the other. These examples of the two kinds of mistakes remind us that internal obstacles tend to be highlighted in those love stories in which the issue is specifically courtship, and often in such narratives my distinction between suitability and difficulty collapses. The question of suitability *is* the difficulty, and the problem (one the characters may be unaware of) is not so much whether two people will be able to get together as whether they belong together in the first place. As such, these plots of internal difficulty are about the anthropological opposite of exogamy: endogamy, or "marriage in." If two people are well suited, then they are marrying within the group whose metaphoric kinship their compatibility represents. But the dark side of courtship is the possibility that it will reveal a mistaken suitability—a nightmare well summarized by Dr. Johnson when he describes a courtship so marked by hypocritical mask-wearing that afterward "each [person] has reason to suspect that some transformation has happened on the wedding night, and that by a strange imposture one has been courted and another married."[5] The Lammles, in Dickens's *Our Mutual Friend*, represent such a courtship brought to married fruition, but the possibility of such a mistake haunts most courtship narratives, and the fear and doubt thus bred compose the obstacles necessary to drive the story along.

Before returning to *Emma*, I wish to make one more point, a historical one. What I have just tried to give is a synchronic summary of the place of obstacles in love stories, but a diachronic influence is at work as well. If we look at erotic narrative over time, what we see is that Adam's line "such as some misfortune brings him, or mistake" works rather like a Janus face, pointing back to a worldview dominated by fortune (and love stories focused almost exclusively on external obstacles) but also pointing forward, to the emerging modern sense of human freedom, wherein the existence of choice always carries with it the possibility of error. It is, I would suggest, only after the true time of Adam's prophecy (the late seventeenth century) that love stories based on internal obstacles emerge on the narrative scene—at about the same time, that is, as the novel itself. And while externalized difficulties like parents and rivals never disappear as a staple item, novels that concern love, especially in England, tend to focus on the kinds of internal problems and questions just discussed. It is, of course, tempting to say that the invention of the novel somehow made it possible to describe states of feeling outside the compass of earlier narrative genres, but I am uncomfortable with the myth of generic progress that such a hypothesis implies. It seems unlikely that Samuel Richardson hit upon a way to describe aspects of human nature that eluded, say, Geoffrey Chaucer, whose *Troilus* also recounts a tale of tragic love. More probably, the novel, with its powerful ability to dissect interior life, appeared when it did because there was a new need to understand human life from the inside out. That demand for interiority seems, to most observers, related to the rise of individualism we observed in the chapter on Defoe and seems ultimately to result in the kind of fiction written by Richardson.

One of the most crucial changes wrought by the new sense of the importance of the individual, especially as it appears in England, was a new ideology of courtship and marriage. These new beliefs have been best summarized in Lawrence Stone's *The Family, Sex, and Marriage in England, 1500–1800,* a work that has been the subject of much praise and blame since its appearance little more than a decade ago.[6] Stone argues that in the seventeenth and eighteenth centuries, England moved from a way of thinking about marriage that was largely dominated by interest (meaning family interests, often financial, and with little regard for the feelings of the prospective mates) to one that was based on choice and the mutual affection of husband and wife—what he calls "the companionate marriage." Some have criticized Stone by insisting that affectionate matches were not as rare in earlier periods as he implies,[7] but whether we grant that assertion or not, Stone's work remains undoubtedly useful as a description of changes in the way marriage was conceptualized and discussed. I would reformulate Stone's argument to say that the change he discusses is a shift in the definition of "likeness," from one in which the terms are largely external to one in which they are primarily internal. Externals like finances and family alliances are supplanted by internal or subjective considerations like temperament and emotions. In such a climate of thought, it follows that the love story itself would change and would do so in a way that Adam's concept of the "mistake" implies. That is, internal obstacles reflect the new companionate ideology. The choice of a mate is largely in the hands of the individual, the suitability of any given partner is a matter of judgment, and—here's the rub—such suitability as married happiness requires may be perceived erroneously. In the old tradition, a bad marriage (or, more broadly, unhappy love) was bad luck (think of Iseult and the love potion), but now it has become one's own fault. The love story has moved inside, and its drama transpires more and more in terms of problems of knowledge. The central problem in examining any relationship becomes "How do I know if this is right?"—with *right* suggesting not so much (or not only) a moral question as an epistemological one: do these feelings reflect correct knowledge?

Quite simply, Jane Austen is the master of this epistemological love story, and all her novels ask the same question: how do we know the human heart? When we enter the world that she creates, we enter a comic world, and so sufficient knowledge is always possible. Otherwise, the order that comedy implies would fail. But because Austen is also a realist, we must also learn that sufficient knowledge is the best we can hope for and is certainly never guaranteed. In *Emma*, problems of knowledge, of both self and other, set in motion a plot that can best be likened to a country dance. Despite the insistence that "five couples are not enough to make [a dance] worth while" (248), we see that three couples—plus Elton, the dangerous extra man—provide Austen with more than enough opportunity to display the full range of possible amatory blunders. It is those blunders which disrupt the stability we observe (or *might* observe, did not our own blunders stand in the way) at the outset of the novel and which thereby set in motion this dancelike plot in which everyone changes partners again and again.[8]

I will not say too much about Harriet Smith and Robert Martin. Martin has only a small role in this dance, sitting out early and resuming his place only at the end. For him, Emma is a blocking figure, and it is her mistaken sense of Harriet's status that stands between his inclination and its reward. Harriet herself is remarkable only for her prettiness and her tractability. She makes a series of mistakes—refusing Martin, aspiring to Elton, and then persisting in that affection long after he has made clear that it is unrequited. Her primary problem, though, is that species of amatory blunder for which Austen's last novel was named, "persuasion." Emma persuades Harriet not to marry Martin and to love Elton instead. But such apparently internal problems are really inside Emma, not Harriet. It is Emma's mistakes—about Harriet's birth, about Elton's feelings—that block her friend's path to the altar. Harriet's mistakes do not so much arise from within her as they are imposed from without (in contrast to the complexity of Anne Eliott's motivation in *Persuasion*), reminding us ironically that there must be some strength of mind and character for internal obstacles to arise. Most readers have noted Emma's tendency to construct romances, populating her tales with the people around her.[9] From this perspective, we could look at Emma's meddling in Harriet's life as an attempt to construct a love story without obstacles. After all, flush with her apparent success in matching the Westons, Emma tells Harriet, "There does seem to be a something in the air of Hartfield which gives love exactly the right direction, and sends it into the very channel where it ought to flow" (75). But she should know better; she has just quoted Shakespeare's own remark on the necessity of difficulty—"The course of true love never did run smooth"—and her behavior with Harriet is a firm reminder that Hartfield is no exception. Inadvertently, what Emma has constructed is a very old-fashioned love story, a tale of two lovers kept apart by misfortune, with herself, the ostensible matchmaker, actually taking on the powerful role of blocking character.

Frank Churchill and Jane Fairfax provide a far more interesting example of and commentary on the traditional love story. Theirs is an embedded narrative, though not in the usual way. We see their story not as a digression from the main narrative (as is the story of Leonora in Fielding's *Joseph Andrews*, for example) but rather as something concealed between the lines. Reading and rereading *Emma* is a little like multiple readings of *Tom Jones*—our initial delight (as with any mystery) is with being taken in, and our repeated pleasure is in observing the skill with which we were duped.[10] The difference—and it is a crucial one—is that the mistakes we make on a first reading of Fielding are the result of the narrator's direct manipulation of information, whereas our errors in perceiving the truth about Frank and Jane arise more indirectly, through our identification with a powerful point-of-view character, Emma herself, whose consciousness so colors the action that even readers who dislike her cannot help but duplicate her mistakes. Thus, in *Emma* we get no such pointed advice as Fielding gives: "If the reader will please to refresh his Memory, by turning to the Scene at *Upton* . . . , he will be apt to admire the many strange Accidents," and so on (916). Instead, we have Frank, in his letter to his stepmother, saying, "[If] you will look back," and so on (437). Austen, that is, controls information as powerfully as Fielding does, but the latter announces his control, whereas Austen keeps herself discreetly out of sight. But the effect is not dissimilar, even if the narrative voices are widely different. The story of Frank and Jane, like the tale of Blifil's duplicity, is always there, but our own inadequacy as readers of experience—which both books make us confront and which in *Emma* serves to ameliorate whatever superiority we may initially feel toward the heroine—blinds us to it.

One result of the revelation of the truth about Frank and Jane at the end of *Emma* is that Austen's novel takes on, retrospectively, the formal pattern so popular in medieval and Renaissance drama, the double plot. Double plots, as Empson has shown so well, work to broaden our sense of the action represented.[11] Gloucester's agony, for example, reminds us that *King Lear* is not merely the story of one family's problems, and Austen's juxtaposition of the story of these two courtships—Frank and Jane, Emma and Knightley—enables her both to survey the whole history of the love story and to comment on two different kinds of love. The Churchill-Fairfax courtship, once revealed, is a very traditional tale. The problem seems to be bad luck (Jane is poor), the resulting obstacles are external, and the plot is a classic tale of family opposition—and one with intriguing overtones of adultery. Jane's relative poverty also suggests the class issue, reminding us once more that external obstacles reflect an erotic world in which the problem is some form of exogamy. Jane is the dangerous outsider, threatening to enter Frank's world.

Briefly, what we learn is that Frank and Jane met at Weymouth, fell in love, and became secretly engaged. The secrecy was necessitated, as Frank puts it in his letter of exculpation (a letter that is, in a way, the plot summary of this other novel that is embedded in *Emma*), because of "my difficulties in the then state of Enscombe" (437), a polite way of saying that his demanding aunt, Mrs. Churchill, would never approve of the match. The couple's response to this misfortune is to keep silent and wait for a change of luck, what Frank calls "time, chance, circumstances, slow effects, sudden bursts, perseverance, and weariness, health and sickness" (437). Frank thus announces explicitly this couple's allegiance to the world of fortune. And after a year's painful concealment, the hoped-for good luck arrives in the form of the death of Mrs. Churchill (who could, like the wit, have carved on her tombstone, "I told you I was sick"). That impediment removed, Frank and Jane are to be married as the novel ends.

To call this story a courtship would be in many ways a misnomer. More accurately, it is the narrative of an awkward space in time, the period between this couple's courtship (which we never see and which ends with their engagement) and their marriage. But in many ways, that is precisely the time frame of the traditional love story, which often begins with some kind of recognition and in which the problem is not knowledge of whom you love but access to each other. The essence of courtship, on the other hand, is some uncertainty of feeling far more than it is availability. But availability is Frank and Jane's problem: like Lancelot and Guinivere, they have a hard time being together. An external obstacle—like a parent or a mate—tends to create physical distance. Jane Eyre, whose story is a fascinating mixture of old and new, must leave Thornfield as soon as she learns of Bertha's existence. Frank and Jane's story, then, as we reconstruct it, is situated in a liminal space, one that is always dangerous, because they are neither independent of each other nor joined together. And while the obstacle is family opposition, what Austen shows us is the way such a situation can become metaphorically, if not literally, adulterous.

To understand how this love appears adulterous, we must consider several points. First is the matter of Mr. Dixon, husband to Jane's friend, the rather plain Miss Campbell. As soon as Jane arrives in Highbury, Emma (apparently unmoved by her recent failure to construct a love story starring Elton and Harriet) begins to fashion a new tale around Jane and Mr. Dixon. Emma's imagination combines the prurient with the moral, and the narrative she manufactures makes Jane guilty of a forbidden longing that she must heroically struggle to repress. Having failed to create a story of happy love, Emma now assembles a tragic one from a few scraps of material—Jane's refusal to go to Ireland, the mysterious arrival of a piano. Of course, Emma is as wrong about Jane's feelings as she was about Elton's, and one point of all these proceedings is to underline Emma's propensity to make mistakes about other people's emotions. But there is another effect, equally important, of her speculation about Mr. Dixon. It casts Jane in an adulterous light from the first time we see her. Her reserve, which Emma finds so obnoxious (she finds it both "disgusting" and "suspicious" [169]), is made to seem the fruit of guilt, not temperament. What we will see is that the guilty light in which Jane first appears is carried over to her relationship with Frank.

Adultery, by definition, implies a triangle and usually secrecy as well. The problems are interrelated—the third party who interferes is also the one who must be kept in the dark. As if to emphasize the way in which traditional love stories tend to rely on triangular structures, with either the rival or the family as the third term, and simultaneously to make fun of that tendency, Austen resorts to a complex proliferation of three-sided relationships with Jane and Frank in the middle. As origin, there is the *senex iratus* herself, Mrs. Churchill, whose existence guarantees that the couple has not "a hope, a chance, a possibility" (398) of union. But that is only the start, and possible triangles multiply comically: Jane loves Mr.

Dixon, but he is married (imagined by Emma); Emma loves Frank, but he loves Jane (imagined by both the Westons and Knightley); Harriet loves Frank, but he loves Jane (Emma, again); Frank flirts with Emma while ignoring Jane (observed by everyone); and Knightley criticizes Emma while praising Jane (especially noted by Mrs. Weston). It is almost as if Frank and Jane use false triangles to disguise the only one among these possibilities that is real, the one they share with Mrs. Churchill. More interesting here than the kind of concealment motivatinng Frank's feigned interest in Emma, however, is the fact that so many of the residents of proper Highbury are ready to perceive romantic triangles at work. When she discovers the truth, Emma bursts out, condemning Jane and Frank for their "system of hypocrisy and deceit,—espionage and treachery" (399) and sounds at that moment very much like a wronged spouse. The irony is that she, and everyone else, has been imagining some such system all along. The effect is to remind us that we all share a tendency to construct this kind of narrative about the love lives of others. Again, Austen does not allow us as readers to feel as superior to Emma as we might like. At the same time, Emma's anger also works to convey again the fact that Jane and Frank's relationship really does have an adulterous feel to it.

I said earlier that, in the abstract, love stories with an external obstacle tend to divide into plots of family opposition and plots of adultery but that, in practice, those two kinds often blend into one. That may seem paradoxical, but Austen's handling of the embedded narrative of Jane and Frank serves to demonstrate how logical the connection really is. Both adultery and marriage without parental consent imply disloyalty to the family—either to the family one has created by an earlier marriage or to the family of birth. In either case, the lover is violating some taboo of exogamy: he or she is going outside limits, either of morality or of class, deemed acceptable by the family. Mrs. Churchill is a perfect character to illustrate this convergence, for she is literally neither mother nor wife to Frank. As an aunt and an older woman, she partakes of the role of mother, but as part of a family bond that has been created (Frank, we must remember, was adopted), she also has something of the flavor of a wife. Her brand of querulous invalidism is also, of course, a staple of plots of adultery in which a husband is trapped not only by marriage but by the illness of his mate—think of Rochester. In loving Jane, Frank violates his loyalty to Mrs. Churchill;

quite simply, he cannot be true to both. In a curious but pronounced way, then, love for someone from a different class reveals itself as adulterous: some vow of fidelity is being broken when a lover steps outside his or her group.

Austen's achievement in telling this story lies in the way she manipulates the discrepancy between the surface facts of Jane and Frank's relationship and the tone those facts suggest. The surface facts are innocent: two young people meet, fall in love, become engaged, and, after a year, marry. In the interim, no one is terribly hurt, and, by our standards anyway, no egregious lies are told. The tone, however, is something else again. Emma's outburst, quoted earlier, reflects the essential innocence of Highbury life but also emphasizes that something that feels really scandalous is going on, a scandal that is remarkably close to adultery, compounded as it is of concealment and disloyalty. Adding to this effect, when the revelations are finally made and all feelings out in the open, the love of Jane and Frank has a sense of the directly sexual about it that is rare in Austen. In the novel's penultimate chapter, Frank and Emma talk about all that has happened. Jane is nearby, and her future husband cannot keep his eyes off her: "Did you ever see such a skin?—such smoothness! . . . Look at her. . . . Observe the turn of her throat. Observe her eyes" (478–79). This kind of emphasis on details of appearance is rare in Austen[12] and often carries connotations of disapproval. I am not sure here that we should see such detail as an implied condemnation of Jane; rather, it seems to deepen the sense Austen created from the start that this is an old-fashioned kind of love story and that its reliance on an external obstacle links it to a tradition of erotic narrative going back to the Middle Ages that tends to be adulterous and more frankly sexual. Many years ago, C. S. Lewis named adultery as one of the four defining characteristics of courtly love.[13] In light of the discussion here, it may be that we can see adultery as not merely a literal fact (e.g., that Guinivere is married to Arthur, or Iseult to Mark) but a metaphor for an erotic psychology in which the obstacle to union is perceived to be in some way "outside" the self.

We can certainly see the struggle of loyalties we observe in a character like Frank as the reflection of a problem of self-knowledge: "Where do I belong?" But I would argue that there is another way to tell a love story, one that attempts to represent an internal problem more directly, and that such a representation becomes more necessary in the wake of the changes in the ideology of marital choice discussed earlier. There is a difference—and a significant one— between divided loyalties and inadequate self-knowledge, and there is a difference in the way the stories of people dealing with those two kinds of problems are told. Jane and Frank illustrate the first; Emma and Knightley embody the second.

As I observed earlier, there is apparently no good reason that Emma and Knightley are not married in chapter 1—a truth Austen herself admits many pages later: "It was a union of the highest promise of felicity . . . , and without one real, rational difficulty to oppose or delay it" (468). Given what I have said about obstacles, then, how do we have a novel at all? The simple answer is that Emma and Knightley were in love but did not know it, a peculiar condition that looks back to *Pamela* (who, apparently perversely, refuses to run away from Mr. B.) and that is the staple plot of Austen's novelistic career. As opposed to old-style love stories, which, as we have seen, begin with the recognition of love, usually love at first sight (Troilus smitten at the window, Anna's fatal glance back at Vronsky on the train), these stories climax with recognition, a situation that demands characters who are ignorant of their own internal state of affairs. At the end of *Pride and Prejudice*, when Elizabeth Bennet asks Darcy when he fell in love, he has to admit that he cannot do it: "I cannot fix on the hour, or the spot, or the look, or the words. . . . I was in the middle before I knew that I *had* begun."[14] This kind of self-ignorance is an emotional problem for the characters, but for readers of Austen, it is also necessary to appreciate that this ignorance is a narrative problem as well. How can such a story be told?

As befits a world in which knowledge is the problem, the basic mode of stories with an internal obstacle is empirical. What we see is a process of coming-to-know, and the acquisition of that knowledge involves a process of testing, error, and ultimate validation. Testing, of course, was present in traditional erotic narrative: Guinivere demands that Lancelot perform badly in the tournament in Chretian's *Lancelot*. But its role there seems bound more to issues of power than to those of discovery. Moreover, the empiricism of *Emma* is as unconscious as the feelings it finally uncovers. It is as if the answer to the danger Dr. Johnson formulated—courtship in disguise—is unconscious courtship. If you don't know what you are doing, you can hardly dissimulate.

Perhaps the most prominent feature of unconscious courtship is the unwitting comparison. As Chapman recognized long ago, Emma is measuring all the men around her against a yardstick named Knightley long before such an idea ever consciously occurs to her.[15] When Mrs. Weston reveals to her the truth about Frank and Jane, Emma blasts that young man with a portrait of masculine rectitude that we, by this point, recognize as Knightley: "So unlike what a man should be!—None of that upright integrity, that strict adherence to truth and principle, that disdain of trick and littleness, which a man should display in every transaction of his life" (397). But the novel is scattered with such passages, places where Knightley's name is elided but his presence is strong: "[Emma] liked [Mr. Weston's] open manners, but a little less of openheartedness would have made him a higher character.—General benevolence, but not general friendship, made a man what he ought to be.—She could fancy such a man" (320). Often, Knightley seems to function rather like the purloined letter—the object of desire rendered invisible simply because it is always in plain sight.

Comparison, of course, implies a triangle, and triangles are as important to the story of Emma and Knightley as they were in that of Jane and Frank—but with one crucial difference. Frank has chosen one triangle, involving Mrs. Churchill and Jane, and he has constructed another, with Emma, purposely to mislead; his triangles, that is, are deliberate. The triangles around Emma and Knightley, on the other hand, are inadvertent or, despite appearances, nonexistent. They tend to promote a process of not concealment but revelation. Here, jealousy is not an obstacle, as it is in any of those relations I have called adulterous, but an ally. For Emma and Knightley, jealousy is no green-eyed monster but a clear-eyed friend, the agent that makes plain sight possible.

As we have seen, there are many triangles in *Emma*, and it would be tedious to pause over each of them. Let us focus instead on what we can call the two revelatory triangles: those formed by Emma and Knightley with first Frank and then Harriet. The first is the agent of Knightley's enlightenment; the second, of Emma's. Because the novel is so dominated by Emma's consciousness, the story of Knightley's triangle, like the story of Jane and Frank, is one we largely reconstruct. Austen gives us the bare facts, and we use them to rearrange and correct our memory of previous events: "[T]here had been a long-standing jealousy, old as the arrival, or even the expectation, of Frank Churchill.—[Knightley] had been in love with Emma, and jealous of Frank Churchill, from about the same period, one sentiment having probably enlightened him as to the other" (432). A little later, Knightley confesses that he has been in love with Emma since she was "thirteen at least" (462), and so we learn that he has been in that peculiar state of unconscious love for six or seven years before Frank wakes him from his amatory slumber. With Emma, the interior detailing is richer, but the pattern is exactly the same. Learning to her shock and chagrin that Harriet is not quite so docile as she imagined and that Harriet has set her mobile sights on Knightley himself, Emma "acknowledged the whole truth. . . . It darted through her, with the speed of an arrow, that Mr. Knightley must marry no one but herself!" (408). And in trying to discover how old this feeling is, she, like Darcy, finds that she cannot fix an origin: "She saw that there never had been a time when she did not consider Mr. Knightley as infinitely the superior [to Frank], or when his regard for her had not been infinitely the most dear" (412).

Emma and Knightley follow a similar process, one of mistake and revelation. The initial mistake is about someone else's feelings, a mistake that creates jealousy, which in turn enlightens both of them about more fundamental mistakes they are making about their own hearts. Until Harriet confesses her hopes for Knightley, Emma "had been totally ignorant of her own heart" (412), a condition that her future husband mirrors. Mistaken self-knowledge thus emerges as the true obstacle to union (as Adam had predicted), but—and here again we confront the fact that Austen's is a comic world—mistakes about others and the jealousy those mistakes provoke ironically become the solution to the problem of self-ignorance. Because this *is* a comedy, however, it is not enough that these characters learn from their mistakes (so does Othello, after all); the mistakes must be revealed as in some way intrinsic to the operation of goodness and order. Milton and the doctrine of the *felix culpa* come to mind—that is, a higher good has been produced because it has been made out of evil, or what passes for evil in the safe confines of Highbury. But while Austen is comic, she is never softheaded and there are limits to what this brand of erotic empiricism can reveal. At the very moment when the plot takes its right-angled turn from mistake to revelation and union, Austen reminds us that we cannot hope for full knowledge; we can only hope for enough: "Seldom, very seldom, does complete truth belong to any human disclosure; seldom can it happen that something is not a little disguised, or a little mistaken; but where, as in this case, though the conduct is mistaken [Austen is referring to Emma's concealment of Harriet's role in the change taking place], the feelings are not, it may not be very material" (431).

We discussed sexuality in relation to Jane and Frank, and it remains to look at the place of sex in a world of internal obstacles such as Emma and Knightley inhabit. The bond they establish has often been considered rather sexless,[16] and Emma's admission, late in the story, that even as his wife she will never be able to call him "George" (463) creates the uncomfortably comic possibility that she will call him "Mr. Knightley" even in bed. There are, however, some things to mitigate this apparent sexlessness. Jealousy itself, so intrinsic to this couple's acts of self-discovery, carries with it an inevitable sexual charge, even in this novel, where its role can seem more empirical than erotic. Too, we must consider the delightful ferocity with which Emma and Knightley speak to each other throughout the novel—a conversational contest marked by the kind of wit and banter we associate with the verbally duelling lovers of the Restoration stage. Emma and Knightley (and Darcy and Elizabeth, for that matter) are, of course, free of the sexual innuendos and license that mark the speech of Harriet and Dorimant or Millamant and Mirabell, and Austen's women certainly have most of the wit, but the energy with which these couples spar serves to sexualize the atmosphere whenever they are together. Emma also admires the way Knightley dances, and good dancing often works as a sexual signal in Austen's novels.[17] But one exchange that occurs when Emma and Knightley dance also points to the problem with their sexuality. As they walk onto the floor, Emma remarks, "[Y]ou know we are not really so much brother and sister as to make [dancing] at all improper," to which Knightley replies, "Brother and sister! no indeed" (331). Despite this explicit and quite-touching denial, however, the old charge of sexlessness does seem to originate here: Emma and Knightley strike many as having a familial rather than a lovers' relationship.

The problem is not that Emma and Knightley seem like brother and sister (though they are siblings by marriage); besides, many of Austen's contemporaries among the romantic poets found that bond peculiarly fraught with erotic possibility. Rather, the difficulty is that they seem a good deal like father and daughter. To call them sexless reflects the disparity in their ages (close to twenty years) and, even more, Knightley's role as instructor and moral guardian to a willful and fallible young woman. Important as those considerations are, however, I think that the question of incest[18] is much more complicated than these explanations suggest, and to appreciate that complexity, we need to reexamine the concept of a person's being in love and not knowing it, a condition that, as we have seen, marks both these lovers. What if we restated the problem this way, as a person's being unaware of his or her own *desire?* The very teleology of desire seems to require an object, and an object that is known, for if desire is founded on absence, how can we be in a state of desire if we are ignorant that such an absence exists?

Freudian psychology suggests one answer: repression. As human beings, we both want and simultaneously refuse to know what we want, because our first object of desire is a forbidden one. That is, incestuous desire is precisely the kind of desire that tends to remain unconscious, and the path to its acknowledgment is blocked by the strongest resistances. To the extent that we are all caught up in the oedipal scenario, we are all in love and all ignorant of that love most of the time. But that ignorance breeds further difficulties, difficulties related to what psychoanalysis calls transference. In a typical transference-love, an individual unconsciously but irresistibly sees the parent in the love object and maps infantile patterns onto adult bonds. As Janet Malcom beautifully describes the theory of transference, "[W]e spend our lives playing out the same internal drama—that of our earliest parental and sibling relationships—indiscriminately casting the people we meet in the leading roles and doing our own rote performance of the part of the child."[19] The adult in search of love, having internalized the image of the parent, finds in the lover a kind of mirror wherein that old secret image can be projected. Thus, even if we know that we are in love, that love is inevitably marked by a mistake—the usual failure to see that the ostensible lover is merely a stand-in, a presence animated for us by the ghost of that first love, the parent.

Emma provides us with an interesting version of this pattern. In one sense, Emma's inability to recognize her feelings for Knightley reflects just this kind of repression. He is far more like a father to her than Mr. Woodhouse, who could hardly be more childlike if he wore a bib and sat in a high chair. And since Knightley is so much like a father, Emma would tend to repress any feeling for him as a violation of taboo. But in this novel, there is also a delicious wish fulfillment worked out, one that reminds us that this is a work of art, not a documentary, and that these are characters, not real people. Because her father represents such a vacuum, the image that Emma has internalized, and thus the image she will seek in a lover, is that of not Mr. Woodhouse but Knightley himself. She can therefore transfer her unconscious desire onto its original source rather than some disappointing substitute. Marriage to Knightley, then, represents a remarkable circumvention of the incest taboo. Emma, lucky girl, gets to have her oedipal cake and eat it too. Such a fantasy is both powerful and frightening, and we can recognize, perhaps, in the refusal of so many readers to acknowledge the sexuality of Emma and Knightley a kind of imposition of the incest taboo on the text. We tend to see their relationship as sexless in part because we prefer to avert our eyes from the possibility that these desires exist, much less that they can be fulfilled. Such perceptions about Austen's hero and heroine may thus be reflective of our own anxieties far more than they are an illustration of the old accusation that Austen lacks passion.

Mr. Woodhouse, lest we gloss over him too quickly, also provides a striking commentary on the kind of external blocking characters so prominent in the traditional love story. Austen establishes a strong parallel between him and Mrs. Churchill: both are demanding, invalidlike, and apparently unwilling to accept the loss of their children to marriage. If anything, Mr. Woodhouse's potential as an obstacle is greater than that of Frank's aunt. Over and over, we hear his feelings about Isabella and about "poor Mrs. Weston," and in the first chapter, we learn that "[m]atrimony . . . was always disagreeable [to him]" (37). When, so belatedly, Emma and Knightley do recognize their feelings, they enter for a time into a kind of secret engagement of their own—secret from her father. Emma's sense, like Frank's, is that as long as her parent lives, she cannot marry (435). But these fears and hesitations prove to be smoke without fire. When finally told the news, Mr. Woodhouse reacts not like a parent but like a disappointed child, resisting change initially but ultimately pliable. He is merely the shadow of a blocking agent and serves as a reminder of another way, the old-fashioned way, in which the story of Emma and Knightley could have been told. As if to emphasize that Mr. Woodhouse's nature is only apparently and not really a problem, Austen tells us that his nerves are in fact what ultimately smooth the way for the wedding to take place: on the novel's last page, we learn that the wedding plans can go forward "not by any sudden illumination of Mr. Woodhouse's mind, or any wonderful change of his nervous system, but by the operation of the same system in another way" (483). He is terrified of chicken thieves and needs a man in the house. The old-fashioned obstacle, it turns out, is a friend.

That phrase—*the operation of the same system in another way*—could serve as a summary of the resolution of the whole plot of this novel. As noted earlier, the household constituted by the concluding marriage is the same one we observe in the book's first pages. Emma and Knightley, to be sure, have become husband and wife and have undergone a long process of illumination, but if we think of the opening and closing as tableaux, we see, as Donne would say, "small change." And this perception reminds us that this new-style love story I have tried to describe is ultimately endogamous in tendency. It serves to recount, that is, the tale of a "marriage in"—a marriage that consolidates a family and violates no group boundaries. As we saw, the old-style love story usually works to set up a choice between incest and adultery, a contest between loyalty to a preexisting group (usually the family but also one's class) and loyalty to a lover outside that circle. Jane and Frank typify that kind of narrative. Emma and Knightley, however, face no such conflict. Their problem is to see that they are, in a profound sense, already together, so that their marriage is not so much the creation of a family as the confirmation of one. As we have seen, such a pattern inevitably carries an incestuous connotation, one emphasized here by the fact that the child, Emma, does not really have to leave her family and cleave unto her husband. When she breaks the news of her engagement, Emma tells her father that "she was not going from Hartfield; she should be always there" (466). Unlike Frank, who had to choose and whose choice required a death, Emma has only to look within herself. Once she does, the course of her love can indeed run smooth.

Conclusion

Samuel Johnson titled the last chapter of *Rasselas* "The Conclusion, in Which Nothing is Concluded" and thereby set a precedent for all writers who wish to finish but are reluctant to provide the kind of assured summary that a "conclusion" can imply. I began this study with the conviction that the eighteenth-century English novel is a remarkably flexible and various form; for me to try now to generalize conclusively about its shape, meaning, or ideology would seem like a contradiction of my primary assumption. Frank Kermode once said that the history of the novel is a history of antinovels,[1] and his comment is illuminating for the novels examined here. It may seem paradoxical to call novels antinovels when the form itself is as fluid as I believe it to have been in the eighteenth century. But if we take *antinovel* more broadly, as suggesting a fiction that attempts to reinvent the possibilities of the form, then all the novels we have looked at here are antinovels, radical fictions that consistently reimagine what a novel might be. The attempt made by many critics to find a defining principle or common origin for these works seems to me to be, as I said at the outset, misleading. The experience of reading eighteenth-century English novels is, among other pleasures, an extended discovery of the apparently limitless possibilities these writers saw inherent in the form.

Having said that, however, I would like to point to a passage in *Emma* that suggests some tendencies in the novel as a genre, tendencies that will have to serve in lieu of a conclusion. Emma and Harriet are shopping at Ford's, and Austen's heroine, bored with her friend's indecision, steps outside to take the air:

Emma went to the door for amusement.—Much could not be hoped from the traffic of even the busiest part of Highbury;—Mr. Perry walking hastily by, Mr. William Cox letting himself in at the office door, Mr. Cole's carriage horses returning from exercise, or a stray letter-boy on an obstinate mule, were the liveliest objects she could presume to expect; and when her eyes fell only on the butcher with his tray, a tidy old woman travelling homewards from shop with her full basket, two curs quarelling over a dirty bone, and a string of dawdling children round the baker's little bow-window eyeing the gingerbread, she knew she had no reason to complain, and was amused enough; quite enough to stand still at the door. A mind lively and at ease, can do with seeing nothing, and can see nothing that does not answer. (233)

It is a striking meditation, a point in the novel where Austen seems to have effaced the difference she usually maintains between herself and Emma. Emma's mind, after all, while lively, is rarely at ease, and she typically seeks stronger amusement than dogs worrying over a bone. If we take the mind at work here, then, to be closer to Austen's than to Emma's usual mental state, we gain a rare glimpse of a novelist's mind at work. And we could abstract that picture to say something like, "The observation of nothing for the sake of amusement." Now by *nothing*, Austen does not seem to mean any literal void (we are still a century away from Stevens's "Snow Man," in which we are enjoined to see "nothing that is not there, / And the nothing that is"). She means something more like what Johnson had in mind when he told Boswell, "There is nothing, Sir, too little for so little a creature as man. It is by studying little things that we attain the great art of having as little misery and as much happiness as possible."[2]

The work of the novelist, then, is the careful observation of little things. But "little things" is a concept that encompasses a great deal. It includes all that particularity—of time, of place, of description, of name, of speech—that Watt thought so important to our sense of the novel;[3] it certainly also implies that attention to the middle and lower classes so often remarked on as novelistic. It calls to mind the ability of the genre, present from the time of Defoe, to observe the familiar and the domestic so closely that the very texture of daily life again becomes strange. But Austen's meditation, though it comprehends all these points very well, suggests more, for the passage not only makes us aware of what Emma might see or did see but also draws our attention to the process of observation itself. We watch her watching, observe her hoping to find— and finding—something to observe. The best eighteenth-century novels are often attentive to both the extraordinary range of "little things" that can be seen and the way in which they are looked at. The process of looking, that is, is another little thing worth looking at.

The aforementioned tendencies in the novel (and they are only tendencies and neither limit the possibilities of the form nor are limited to it; other art both observes and explains) can be laid at the door of any one of a number of usual suspects: Locke's empirical psychology, the rise of individualism, Puritan introspection, the breakdown of a deferential social order, the growth of the middle class. But the responsibility is less important than the consequences. Wherever they learned it, the early writers of English novels knew that one really could put anything in a novel, that all the "little things" of life were more than enough. "Trifles light as air" have, of course, always been a part of narrative art, but never until the arrival of the novel in the eighteenth century were they found by so many to be so consistently (to use Austen's word) amusing, were they believed to be (as Johnson implies) so decisively instructive. A footprint. A maidenhead. An orphan's last name. An unwound clock. A statue on a tomb. A neighborhood dance. "She knew"—as should we all—"that she had no reason to complain."

Notes and References

INTRODUCTION

1. Daniel Defoe, *The Life and Strange Surprizing Adventures of Robinson Crusoe . . .* , ed. Donald J. Crowley (Oxford: Oxford University Press, 1981), 53; Samuel Richardson, *Clarissa, or The History of a Young Lady,* ed. John Butt, 4 vols. (New York: Dutton; London: Dent, 1932; reprint, 1962), 3: 210; Henry Fielding, *The History of Tom Jones, a Foundling,* ed. Martin Battestin and Fredson Bowers (Middletown, Conn.: Wesleyan University Press, 1975), 154; Laurence Sterne, *The Life and Opinions of Tristram Shandy, Gentleman,* ed. Melvyn New and Joan New (Gainesville: University of Florida Press, 1978), 248; Horace Walpole, *The Castle of Otranto,* ed. W. S. Lewis (Oxford: Oxford University Press, 1982), 102; *Emma,* in *The Novels of Jane Austen,* ed. R. W. Chapman, 5 vols. (Oxford: Oxford University Press, 1923; reprint, 1960), 4: 323. Unless otherwise noted, all parenthetical references in the text are to these editions.

2. *Reflections on the Death of a Porcupine and Other Essays* (Bloomington: Indiana University Press, 1963), 103.

3. Michael McKeon, *The Origins of the English Novel, 1600–1740* (Baltimore and London: Johns Hopkins University Press, 1987), 21.

4. The inability of readers to appreciate fully both Richardson and Fielding is a commonplace criticism of the eighteenth-century novel that is as old as Dr. Johnson. The modern critic who has been most chastised for an inability to comprehend both writers is Ian Watt, whose influential study, many believe, slights the achievement of Fielding. See *The Rise of the Novel: Studies in Defoe, Richardson, and Fielding* (Berkeley and Los Angeles: University of California Press, 1957). See also Watt's marvelous, witty response to his critics, "Serious Reflections on *The Rise of the Novel*," *Novel* 1 (Spring 1968): 205–18.

5. *Johnson's Dictionary, a Modern Selection,* ed. E. L. McAdam, Jr., and George Milne (New York: Pantheon, 1963), 267.

6. Robert D. Hume, "Recent Studies in the Restoration and Eighteenth Century," *Studies in English Literature* 28 (Summer 1988): 529.

7. *The New Eighteenth Century: Theory, Politics, English Literature,* ed. Felicity Nussbaum and Laura Brown (New York: Methuen, 1987).

8. T. C. Duncan Eaves and Ben D. Kimpel, *Samuel Richardson: A Biography* (Oxford: Clarendon Press, 1971), 258.

CHAPTER 1

1. To choose only two from among many, see Watt, *The Rise of the Novel,* and Leopold Damrosch, Jr., *God's Plot and Man's Stories: Studies in the*

132

Fictional Imagination from Milton to Fielding (Chicago: University of Chicago Press, 1985). Damrosch explicitly calls *Crusoe* "the first English novel" (187).

2. Northrop Frye, *Anatomy of Criticism: Four Essays* (Princeton, N.J.: Princeton University Press, 1957), 33–34.

3. Watt discusses this issue at length in his chapter "*Robinson Crusoe,* Individualism and the Novel," in *The Rise of the Novel,* 60–92. The relation between individualism and the appearance of the novel also forms one of the many threads in McKeon's *The Origins of the English Novel.*

4. Samuel Taylor Coleridge, *Collected Marginalia,* ed. G. Whalley, 2 vols. (Princeton, N.J.: Princeton University Press, 1984), 2: 116.

5. *Steele's "The Englishman,"* ed. Rae Blanchard (Oxford: Clarendon Press, 1955), no. 26 (3 December 1713), 106–9.

6. Daniel J. Boorstin, *The Image: A Guide to Pseudo-Events in America* (New York: Harper & Row, 1964), 57.

7. See Damrosch's chap. 3, "Art and Truth in *Paradise Lost,*" in *God's Plot and Man's Stories,* esp. p. 120.

8. Watt, *The Rise of the Novel,* 137.

9. Ibid., 71.

10. For more on this issue, see James Nohrnberg, "The *Iliad,*" in *Homer to Brecht: The European Epic and Dramatic Tradition,* ed. Michael Seidel and Edward Mendelson (New Haven, Conn., and London: Yale University Press, 1977), 3.

11. John Richetti makes a similar point in his marvelous *Defoe's Narratives: Situations and Structures* (Oxford: Clarendon Press, 1975). I have been much influenced by Richetti's discussion, especially on the issue of "mastery."

12. For thorough, modern discussions of the religious—and specifically Puritan—elements in *Crusoe,* see Damrosch, *God's Plot and Man's Stories,* and J. Paul Hunter, *The Reluctant Pilgrim: Defoe's Emblematic Method and Quest for Form in "Robinson Crusoe"* (Baltimore: Johns Hopkins University Press, 1966).

13. *The Protestant Ethic and the Spirit of Capitalism,* trans. Talcott Parsons (New York: Charles Scribner's & Sons, 1930), esp. chap. 4 and 5.

14. Watt, *The Rise of the Novel,* 63. For more on Defoe's economics, see Maximilian Novak, *Economics and the Fiction of Daniel Defoe* (Berkeley and Los Angeles: University of California Press, 1962).

15. Richetti, *Defoe's Narratives,* 60.

16. Leslie Stephen, "Defoe's Novels," in *Hours in a Library,* 4 vols. (New York and London: Putnam's, 1904), 1: 52.

17. Marthe Robert, *Origins of the Novel,* trans. Sacha Rabinovitz (Bloomington: Indiana University Press, 1980), 81–104; Emily Brontë, *Wuthering Heights* (Oxford: Clarendon Press, 1975), 72.

18. For these remarks, see Michael Shinagel's edition of *Robinson Crusoe* (New York: Norton, 1975), 282, 292, 294.

19. Ernest Becker, *The Denial of Death* (New York: Free Press, 1973), 36. Damrosch makes a similar point in *God's Plot and Man's Stories,* 196.

20. Ortega y Gasset, *The Revolt of the Masses* (New York: Norton, 1957), 157.

21. George Eliot, *Middlemarch* (Harmondsworth, England: Penguin, 1965), 25.

CHAPTER 2

1. The Butt edition is cited herein; see also *Clarissa, or The History of a Young Lady,* ed. Angus Ross (Harmondsworth, England: Penguin, 1985), and ed. and abr. George Sherburn (Boston: Houghton Mifflin, 1962). Unless otherwise noted, all parenthetical citations in the text are to Butt's edition. References to Ross's edition are cited as "Ross."

2. William Beatty Warner, *Reading "Clarissa": The Struggles of Interpretation* (New Haven, Conn., and London: Yale University Press, 1979), viii. Warner's work has been very influential for me, and it would be both tedious and impossible to note all the instances where our arguments either converge or diverge.

3. See Ross, preface, 9.

4. *An Apology for the Life of Mrs. Shamela Andrews,* ed. Martin Battestin, (Boston: Houghton Mifflin, 1961), 305.

5. See Christopher Hill, "Clarissa Harlowe and Her Times," reprinted in *Puritanism and Revolution* (New York: Schocken, 1958); see also Mark Kinkead-Weekes, *Samuel Richardson, Dramatic Novelist* (Ithaca, N.Y.: Cornell University Press, 1973), 131ff.

6. Claude Lévi-Strauss, *The Elementary Structures of Kinship,* rev. ed., trans. J. H. Bell et al. (Boston: Beacon Press, 1969).

7. Hill, "Clarissa Harlowe and Her Times," 374, 383.

8. A fascinating perspective on the connection of incest and power has recently been advanced by W. Arens in *The Original Sin* (Oxford: Oxford University Press, 1986). Arens argues that, far from being "natural," incest is a specifically cultural activity, one designed to demonstrate the power of those who commit it. The Harlowes, it seems to me, are trying to prove their dominance over their daughter and their independence of the system of exchange.

9. The phrase *uncensored appetites* is Tony Tanner's; see his *Adultery in the Novel* (Baltimore: Johns Hopkins University Press, 1979), 104. Others who remark on Lovelace's sensuality include Margaret Doody, *A Natural Passion: A Study of the Novels of Samuel Richardson* (Oxford: Clarendon Press, 1974), 111; Watt, *The Rise of the Novel,* 237; and Jean Hagstrum, *Sex and Sensibility* (Chicago: University of Chicago Press, 1980), 209.

10. V. S. Pritchett, *"Clarissa,"* in *The Living Novel* (New York: Vintage, 1967), 15.

11. Bernard Mandeville, *A Modest Defense of Publick Stews* (Los Angeles: Augustan Reprint Society, 1973), 37.

12. "The Double Standard," *Journal of the History of Ideas* 20 (1959): 195–216.

13. James Boswell, *The Life of Samuel Johnson,* ed. G. B. Hill and L. F. Powell, 6 vols. (Oxford: Clarendon Press, 1934), 5: 209; see also 2: 457.

14. For some interesting comments on rape versus seduction, see Elizabeth Hardwick, *Seduction and Betrayal* (New York: Random House, 1974), 177.

15. Susan Brownmiller, *Against Our Will: Men, Women, and Rape* (New York: Simon and Schuster, 1975), 5.

16. See, for instance, Watt, *The Rise of the Novel*, 237.

17. *Johnsonian Miscellanies*, ed. G. B. Hill, 2 vols. (Oxford: Clarendon Press, 1897), 1: 297.

18. For a thorough feminist reading of the novel, see Terry Castle, *Clarissa's Cyphers: Meaning and Disruption in Richardson's "Clarissa"* (Ithaca, N.Y., and London: Cornell University Press, 1982).

19. For discussions of the death, see Doody, *A Natural Passion*, 171; Kinkead-Weekes, *Samuel Richardson*, 267–72; and Ann Barton, "What's a Girl to Do?" *New York Review of Books*, 21 July 1983, 32.

20. Examples of Richardson-as-Puritan arguments can be found in Watt, *The Rise of the Novel*; Pritchett, *"Clarissa"*; and Cynthia Woolf, *Samuel Richardson and the Eighteenth-Century Puritan Character* (Hampden, Conn.: Archon Books, 1972).

21. Contrast, on this point, Castle, who says that Clarissa's death represents a "methodical self-expulsion from the realm of signification" (109).

22. *Selected Letters of Samuel Richardson*, ed. John Carroll (Oxford: Clarendon Press, 1964), 73, 113, and *The Correspondence of Samuel Richardson*, ed. Anna Laetitia Barbauld, 6 vols. (New York: AMS Press, 1966), 4: 181.

23. *"Clarissa's* Richardson," in *English Literature in the Age of Disguise*, ed. Maximillian Novak (Berkeley: University of California Press, 1977), 157.

24. *Modern Critical Views: Samuel Richardson*, ed. Harold Bloom (New York: Chelsea House, 1987), 1.

25. Carroll, *Selected Letters*, 144.

26. See esp. Warner, *Reading "Clarissa"*; Castle, *Clarissa's Cyphers*; and Terry Eagleton, *The Rape of Clarissa: Writing, Sexuality, and Class Struggle in Samuel Richardson* (Oxford and London: Basil Blackwell, 1982).

CHAPTER 3

1. For more on Fielding and language, see also Glenn W. Hatfield, *Henry Fielding and the Language of Irony* (Chicago and London: University of Chicago Press, 1968). Hatfield generally construes the term *language* more narrowly than I do here and concentrates on mostly verbal effects. He also usefully surveys Fielding's thinking about language and its abuses in his other work, including the journalism. Martin Price's discussion of the "subversion of forms" in Fielding is also related to the argument I make here. See Price's *To the Palace of Wisdom: Studies in Order and Energy from Dryden to Blake* (Carbondale and Edwardsville: Southern Illinois University Press, 1964; reprint, 1970), 293–304.

2. See Wayne Booth, *The Rhetoric of Fiction* (Chicago: University of Chicago Press, 1961), 215–18.

3. Robert Alter's *Fielding and the Nature of the Novel* (Cambridge, Mass.: Harvard University Press, 1968) is excellent on Fielding's tendency to parallel scenes late in the novel with actions that occur toward the beginning; see esp. pp. 117f.

4. On this tendency, Ronald Paulson says, "While [Pope and Swift] attack the ridiculous behavior in which vanity manifests itself, Fielding attacks the invisible motives in apparently proper behavior. This amounts, finally, to an attack on the reality beneath the card-game of Augustan form." See *Satire and the Novel in Eighteenth-Century England* (New Haven, Conn.: Yale University Press, 1967), 134.

5. As Alter puts it, in his perceptive discussion of the scene, "This entire passage . . . is stylized" (*Fielding and the Nature of the Novel*, 51).

6. My argument here offers an alternative to the traditional speculation that Fielding was originally working with another time scheme and that he changed the chronology of the novel in order to incorporate the Jacobite invasion of 1745–46. See Battestin's notes to pp. 255 and 368 of the Wesleyan edition and his comment in the introduction to that volume, p. xix.

7. For a longer study of *Tom Jones* and literary romance, though one that does not make this point, see Henry Knight Miller, *Henry Fielding's "Tom Jones" and the Romance Tradition* (Victoria, B.C.: English Literary Studies, 1976).

8. Lacan's ideas are by now, of course, widely dispersed through the intellectual community. One good introduction and an unusually lucid one is Malcom Bowie's chapter in *Structuralism and Since: From Lévi-Strauss to Derrida*, ed. John Sturrock (Oxford and New York: Oxford University Press, 1979), 116–53.

9. Paulson's comments on hypocrisy in the novel are particularly good; see *Satire and the Novel*, 136f.

10. For more on Allworthy, see John Preston, *The Created Self: The Reader's Role in Eighteenth-Century Fiction* (London: Heineman, 1970), 124f.

11. Compare, on this point, Watt's belief that what we find in Fielding is a "realism of assessment"—I take his meaning to be in part that Fielding's methods as a novelist force us as readers into a "realistic" position as far as our ability to judge is concerned (*The Rise of the Novel*, 188). Preston develops this point at considerable length; see *The Created Self*, 94–113.

12. Alter is especially shrewd on this aspect of *Tom Jones*; see *Fielding and the Nature of the Novel*, 24, 32.

13. Preston is good on the suspicion we should feel for the narrator and his plot making; see *The Created Self*, 100–1.

14. Here I quote Battestin's commentary in the note on p. 36 of the Wesleyan edition. He develops his argument about the role of prudence in the novel at much greater length in *The Providence of Wit* (Oxford: Clarendon Press, 1974), 116–78.

15. *Tom Jones*, 36n; see also the note on p. 141. Hatfield also develops the difference between true and false prudence; see *Henry Fielding and the Language of Irony*, chap. 5, esp. p. 191.

16. *Rambler*, no. 4 (31 March 1750), in *Samuel Johnson: Selected Poetry and*

Prose, ed. Frank Brady and W. K. Wimsatt (Berkeley and Los Angeles: University of California Press, 1977), 155–59. Johnson never mentions either Fielding or *Tom Jones* by name in this famous discussion of the perils and pleasures of realistic fiction, but it is clear that he has the recently published *Tom Jones* in mind and that he finds Fielding's use of characters who mix good and bad qualities to be dangerous.

17. For the most thorough defense of this position, see *The Providence of Wit,* chap. 5, "Fielding: The Argument of Design." Battestin's arguments in this study have been subjected to rigorous scrutiny by Claude Rawson; see *Order from Confusion Sprung: Studies in Eighteenth-Century Literature from Swift to Cowper* (London: George Allen & Unwin, 1985), 383–402. For another view of Fielding's place in a tradition of providential literature, see Damrosch, chap. 7, "*Tom Jones* and the Farewell to Providential Fiction," in *God's Plot and Man's Stories.*

CHAPTER 4

1. Dedication to vol. 1: "To the Right Honourable Mr. Pitt."

2. Samuel Johnson, *The Lives of the English Poets,* 2 vols. (New York: Dutton, 1925), 2: 204, 264.

3. Philip Dormer Stanhope, *Lord Chesterfield's Letters to His Son (and Others)* (New York: Dutton, 1929), 49.

4. *The English Works of Thomas Hobbes,* ed. Sir William Molesworth, 11 vols. (London: John Bohn, 1839–45), 4:46.

5. Cited in W. A. Speck, *Stability and Strife: England, 1714–1760* (Cambridge, Mass.: Harvard University Press, 1979), 116.

6. Richard A. Lanham, *"Tristram Shandy": The Games of Pleasure* (Berkeley and Los Angeles: University of California Press, 1973), 13.

7. For a more detailed survey of the movement, see Janet Todd, *Sensibility: An Introduction* (London and New York: Methuen, 1986); Ian Watt's discussion in the introduction to his edition of *Tristram Shandy* (Boston: Houghton Mifflin, 1965) is also very good.

8. This image is cited by many of Richardson's critics. See Damrosch, *God's Plot and Man's Stories,* 14. For Hazlitt on Toby, see *Sterne: The Critical Heritage,* ed. Alan B. Howes (London and Boston: Routledge & Kegan Paul, 1974), 361.

9. See Martin Battestin, *The Moral Basis of Fielding's Art: A Study of "Joseph Andrews"* (Middletown, Conn.: Wesleyan University Press, 1959).

10. Laurence Sterne, *A Sentimental Journey through France and Italy* (Harmondsworth, England: Penguin, 1967), 141.

11. Preston, *The Created Self,* 147.

12. See Todd, *Sensibility,* 21.

13. Mikhail Bakhtin, *Rabelais and His World,* trans. Helene Iswolsky (Bloomington: Indiana University Press, 1984). All parenthetical references in the text are to this edition. The most thorough application of Bakhtin to eighteenth-century literature (though one that does not say much about Sterne and the carnivalesque) is Terry Castle's *Masquerade and Civilization:*

The Carnivalesque in Eighteenth-Century Culture and Fiction (Stanford, Calif.: Stanford University Press, 1986).

14. Max Byrd, *"Tristram Shandy"* (London: George Allen & Unwin, 1985), 58. This point is argued fully in John Traugott's *Tristram Shandy's World: Sterne's Philosophical Rhetoric* (Berkeley and Los Angeles: University of California Press, 1954). Traugott is especially good on the trap of language.

15. J. Huizinga, *In the Shadow of Tomorrow;* cited in Lanham, *"Tristram Shandy,"* 42.

16. *Life of Johnson*, 2: 175.

17. Cited in Byrd, *"Tristram Shandy,"* 14.

18. Becker, *The Denial of Death*, 42–46.

19. *Jokes and Their Relation to the Unconscious*, vol. 8 of *The Standard Edition of the Complete Psychological Works of Sigmund Freud*, ed. James Strachey, 24 vols. (London: Hogarth, 1953–74).

20. Freud, *Jokes*, 100.

21. See Richard Ellmann, *Oscar Wilde* (New York: Alfred Knopf, 1988), 469.

22. Preston, *The Created Self*, 159.

23. Freud, *Jokes*, 138–39n.

24. For the argument that Sterne did in fact finish *Tristram Shandy*, see Wayne Booth, "Did Sterne Complete *Tristram Shandy?"* *Modern Philology* 47 (February 1951): 172–83.

CHAPTER 5

1. Samuel Taylor Coleridge, *Biographia Literaria*, ed. Walter J. Bate and James Engell, 2 vols. (Princeton, N.J.: Princeton University Press, 1983), 2: 6.

2. Among recent work, see, for instance, Judith Wilt, *Ghosts of the Gothic: Austen, Eliot, and Lawrence* (Princeton, N.J.: Princeton University Press, 1980), 25, 31; Elizabeth Napier, *The Failure of Gothic: Problems of Disjunction in an Eighteenth-Century Literary Form* (Oxford: Clarendon Press, 1987), chap. 3, "Frenzy: *The Castle of Otranto"*; and Robert Kiely, *The Romantic Novel in England* (Cambridge, Mass.: Harvard University Press, 1972), 33f.

3. Leslie Fiedler, *Love and Death in the American Novel*, rev. ed. (New York: Stein and Day, 1975), 131.

4. *The Yale Edition of Horace Walpole's Correspondence*, ed. W. S. Lewis et al., 48 vols. (New Haven, Conn.: Yale University Press, 1937–83), 3: 260. Further references to Walpole's letters are cited parenthetically in the text as *Correspondence*.

5. What political commentary there has been is well summarized by David Punter, *The Literature of Terror: A History of Gothic Fictions from 1765 to the Present Day* (London and New York: Longman, 1980), 15f. Punter's book is an excellent corrective to this general absence. See also Ronald Paulson, *Representations of Revolution (1789–1820)* (New Haven, Conn.: Yale University Press, 1983).

6. This tendency has been usefully critiqued by Eve Kosofsky Sedg-

wick, "The Character in the Veil: Imagery of the Surface in the Gothic Novel," *PMLA* 96 (March 1981): 255–70.

7. I have in mind Paul Ricoeur's description of the Freudian project as a "hermeneutics of suspicion." See *Freud and Philosophy: An Essay on Interpretation*, trans. Denis Savage (New Haven, Conn.: Yale University Press, 1970), 32f.

8. My understanding of royal effigies is indebted to three works: Ralph E. Giesey, *The Royal Funeral Ceremony in Renaissance France* (Geneva: Librairie E. Droz, 1960); Claire Gittings, *Death, Burial, and the Individual in Early Modern England* (London and Sydney: Croom and Helm, 1984); and Richard Huntington and Peter Metcalf, *Celebrations of Death* (Cambridge: Cambridge University Press, 1979).

9. Ernst H. Kantorowicz, *The King's Two Bodies: A Study in Medieval Political Theology* (Princeton, N.J.: Princeton University Press, 1957), 421.

10. For more on transitions, see Arnold Van Gennep, *The Rites of Passage*, trans. Monika Vizedom and Gabrielle Caffee (Chicago: University of Chicago Press, 1960).

11. Gittings, *Death, Burial, and the Individual*, 216.

12. Giesey, *The Royal Funeral Ceremony*, 164f.

13. C. S. Lewis, *Hamlet: The Prince or the Poem?* (London: British Academy, 1942), 18.

14. Sedgwick's discussion in "The Character in the Veil" centers on Lewis and Radcliffe, but her remarks refer to Gothic fiction generally.

15. *The Sovereignty of the Law: Selections from Blackstone's "Commentaries on the Laws of England,"* ed. Gareth Jones (Toronto: University of Toronto Press, 1973), 100. All parenthetical references in the text to Blackstone are to this edition.

16. Gittings, *Death, Burial, and the Individual*, 228.

17. James Sutherland, *Background for Queen Anne* (London: Methuen, 1939), 215, 220.

18. For accounts of this period, see G. V. Bennett, "Jacobitism and the Rise of Walpole," in *Historical Perspectives: Studies in English Thought and Society in Honour of J. H. Plumb*, ed. Neil McKendrick (London: Europa Publications, 1974), and W. A. Speck, *Stability and Strife*, chaps. 9 and 10.

19. For a critical account of Walpole's tactics and personality, see E. P. Thompson, *Whigs and Hunters: The Origin of the Black Act* (New York: Pantheon, 1975). He calls Walpole "England's first and least lovely prime minister" (198). To balance this view, one should consult the standard (if incomplete) biography, J. H. Plumb, *Sir Robert Walpole*, 2 vols. (London: Cresset Press, 1956–60).

20. For a very traditional Freudian/Oedipal reading of *Otranto*, with no political overtones, see Martin Kallich, *Horace Walpole* (New York: Twayne, 1971), 103.

CHAPTER 6

1. Plato, *The Symposium*, trans. Walter Hamilton (Harmondsworth, England: Penguin, 1951), 77.

2. "On the Universal Tendency to Debasement in the Sphere of Love," *Standard Edition*, 11: 187.

3. For an account of adultery and the novel from a rather different perspective, one emphasizing the European tradition of the novel of love, see Tony Tanner, *Adultery in the Novel*.

4. James's quote is "Never say you know the last word about any human heart." Cited in Maynard Mack, *Alexander Pope, a Life* (New Haven, Conn., and London: Yale University Press, 1985), vi.

5. *Rambler* no. 45 (21 August 1750), in *Samuel Johnson: Selected Poetry and Prose*, ed. Frank Brady and W. K. Wimsatt (Berkeley and Los Angeles: University of California Press, 1977), 177.

6. Lawrence J. Stone, *The Family, Sex, and Marriage in England, 1500–1800* (London: Weidenfield and Nicolson, 1977). See esp. chap. 7, "Mating Arrangements," and chap. 8, "The Companionate Marriage."

7. See, for instance, Alan MacFarlane, *Marriage and Love in England, 1300–1800* (Oxford: Basil Blackwell, 1986); as his title suggests, MacFarlane's book attempts to cover much the same ground as Stone's does but takes the view that "love" and affection were common long before Stone would allow. An interesting discussion of the issues of marriage in Austen, seen from a historical viewpoint, can be found in James Thompson, *Between Self and World: The Novels of Jane Austen* (University Park, Pa., and London: Pennsylvania State University Press, 1988), chap. 5, "Courtship, Marriage, and Work."

8. Most critics of Austen have at least touched on the subject of love and marriage; for one commonsensical treatment of the subject, see Juliet McMaster, *Jane Austen on Love* (Victoria, B.C.: English Literary Studies, 1978).

9. An especially good treatment of Emma's proto-novelistic mind is Barbara Hardy's in her *A Reading of Jane Austen* (London: Peter Owen, 1975), 85–86. She does limit the scope of the comparison, insisting that "Jane Austen never writes a novel about a novelist" (85).

10. See note 12 to chapter 3.

11. William Empson, *Some Versions of Pastoral: A Study of Pastoral Form in Literature* (London: Chatto & Windus, 1935), chap. 2, "Double Plots."

12. Irvin Ehrenpreis, *Acts of Implication: Suggestion and Covert Meaning in the Works of Dryden, Pope, Swift, and Austen* (Berkeley and Los Angeles: University of California Press, 1980), 122, 129–30.

13. C. S. Lewis, *The Allegory of Love: A Study in Medieval Tradition* (Oxford: Oxford University Press, 1936), 1, 13–14.

14. *The Novels of Jane Austen*, 2: 380.

15. Ibid., 4: 491–92.

16. Charlotte Brontë is perhaps the most notorious critic of Austen's emotional coolness; she commented in a letter of 1850 that "the Passions are perfectly unknown to her." Cited in *Jane Austen: The Critical Heritage*, ed. B. C. Southam (New York: Barnes and Noble, 1968), 128.

17. See the discussion of Alice Chandler, " 'A Pair of Fine Eyes': Jane Austen's Treatment of Sex," *Studies in the Novel* 7 (Spring 1975): 94–96.

18. An early, intelligent broaching of the subject of incest in Austen, *Mansfield Park* in particular, was made by R. F. Brissenden, *"Mansfield Park: Freedom and the Family,"* in *Jane Austen: Bicentenary Essays,* ed. John Halperin (Cambridge and New York: Cambridge University Press, 1975), 156–71.

19. Janet Malcom, "The Patient Is Always Right," *New York Review of Books,* 20 December 1984, 13. Freud himself puts it more prosaically: "The husband is almost always so to speak only a substitute, never the right man." See "The Taboo of Virginity," *Standard Edition,* 11: 203.

CONCLUSION

1. Frank Kermode, *The Sense of an Ending: Studies in the Theory of Fiction* (New York: Oxford University Press, 1967), 131.

2. Boswell, *The Life of Samuel Johnson,* 1: 433.

3. Watt, Ch. I: "Realism and the Novel Form," in *The Rise of the Novel.*

Selected Bibliography

Primary Works

The date of original publication for each novel is given, followed by the most accessible current edition.

AUSTEN, JANE

The Novels of Jane Austen. Oxford: Oxford University Press, 1923; reprint, 1960.
———. *Emma.* 1815. New York: Norton, 1972.
———. *Mansfield Park.* 1814. Oxford and New York: Oxford University Press, 1980.
———. *Northanger Abbey.* 1818. Harmondsworth, England: Penguin, 1972.
———. *Persuasion.* 1818. Harmondsworth, England: Penguin, 1965.
———. *Pride and Prejudice.* 1813. Harmondsworth, England: Penguin, 1972.
———. *Sense and Sensibility.* 1811. Oxford and New York: Oxford University Press, 1980.

BURNEY, FANNY

Camilla, or A Picture of Youth. 1796. London and New York: Oxford University Press, 1972.
———. *Cecilia, or Memoirs of an Heiress.* 1782. Oxford and New York: Oxford University Press, 1988.
———. *Evelina, or The History of a Young Lady's Entrance into the World.* 1778. London and New York: Oxford University Press, 1968.

CLELAND, JOHN

Memoirs of a Woman of Pleasure. 1748. Oxford and New York: Oxford University Press, 1985.

DEFOE, DANIEL

The Fortunes and Misfortunes of the Famous Moll Flanders. . . . 1722. London and New York: Oxford University Press, 1971.
———. *The History and Remarkable Life of the Truly Honourable Col. Jacque. . . .* 1722. London and New York: Oxford University Press, 1965.
———. *The Journal of the Plague Year. . . .* 1722. London and New York: Oxford University Press, 1969.

————. *The Life, Adventures, and Pyracies of the Famous Captain Singleton.* . . . 1720. London: Oxford University Press, 1969.

————. *The Life and Strange Surprizing Adventures of Robinson Crusoe.* . . . 1719. London and New York: Oxford University Press, 1972.

————. *Roxana, the Fortunate Mistress.* . . . 1724. Oxford and New York: Oxford University Press, 1969.

EDGEWORTH, MARIA

Castle Rackrent. 1800. London and New York: Oxford University Press, 1964.

FIELDING, HENRY

Amelia. 1751. Middletown, Conn.: Wesleyan University Press, 1984.

————. *The History of Tom Jones, a Foundling.* 1749. Middletown, Conn.: Wesleyan University Press, 1975.

————. *Joseph Andrews* and *Shamela.* 1742 and 1741. Boston: Houghton Mifflin, 1961.

GODWIN, WILLIAM

Caleb Williams. 1795. London and New York: Oxford University Press, 1970.

LENNOX, CHARLOTTE

The Female Quixote, or The Adventures of Arabella. 1752. London and New York: Oxford University Press, 1970.

LEWIS, MATTHEW

The Monk, a Romance. 1796. London: Oxford University Press, 1973.

MACKENZIE, HENRY

The Man of Feeling. 1771. London and New York: Oxford University Press, 1970.

RADCLIFFE, ANN

The Italian, or The Confessional of the Black Penitents: A Romance. 1797. London and New York: Oxford University Press, 1968.

————. *The Mysteries of Udolpho: A Romance.* 1794. London and New York: Oxford University Press, 1970.

RICHARDSON, SAMUEL

Clarissa, or The History of a Young Lady. 1747–48. Edited by John Butt. London: Dent and New York: Dutton, 1932; reprint, 1962. Generally follows third edition (1751).

————. *Clarissa, or The History of a Young Lady.* Edited by Angus Ross. Harmondsworth, England: Penguin, 1985. Corresponds to first edition (1747–48).

————. *Clarissa, or The History of a Young Lady.* Edited by George Sherburn. Boston: Houghton Mifflin, 1962. Abridged.

————. *The History of Sir Charles Grandison.* 1753–54. London and New York: Oxford University Press, 1972.

————. *Pamela, or Virtue Rewarded.* 1740–41. London: Dent; New York: Dutton, 1962.

SMOLLETT, TOBIAS

The Adventures of Ferdinand, Count Fathom. 1753. London and New York: Oxford University Press, 1971.

————. *The Adventures of Peregrine Pickle.* 1751. London and New York: Oxford University Press, 1964.

————. *The Adventures of Roderick Random.* 1748. Oxford and New York: Oxford University Press, 1979.

————. *The Expedition of Humphry Clinker.* 1771. London and New York: Oxford University Press, 1966.

————. *The Life and Adventures of Sir Lancelot Greaves.* 1762. London and New York: Oxford University Press, 1973.

STERNE, LAURENCE

The Life and Opinions of Tristram Shandy, Gentleman. 1760–67. Gainesville: University of Florida Press, 1978.

————. *A Sentimental Journey through France and Italy.* 1768. London and Harmondsworth, England: Penguin, 1967.

WALPOLE, HORACE

The Castle of Otranto: a Gothic Story. 1764. London and New York: Oxford University Press, 1964.

Secondary Works

Because this is already a "selected" bibliography, I have included only those works which I consider useful and so have dispensed with evaluative annotation.

GENERAL

BIBLIOGRAPHIES

Glock, Waldo S. *Eighteenth-Century English Literary Studies: A Bibliography.* Metuchen, N.J. and London: Scarecrow Press, 1984.

Watson, George, ed. *The New Cambridge Bibliography of English Literature,* vol. 2, *1660–1800*. Cambridge: Cambridge University Press, 1971. See columns 865–1014.

CRITICAL STUDIES

Booth, Wayne. *The Rhetoric of Fiction*. Chicago: University of Chicago Press, 1961.

Damrosch, Leopold, Jr. *God's Plots and Man's Stories: Studies in the Fictional Imagination from Milton to Fielding*. Chicago: University of Chicago Press, 1985.

———, ed. *Modern Essays on Eighteenth-Century Literature*. Oxford and New York: Oxford University Press, 1988. Not devoted exclusively to the novel, but includes essays on most of the novels surveyed here, as well as others.

McKeon, Michael. *The Origins of the English Novel, 1600–1740*. Baltimore: Johns Hopkins University Press, 1986.

Preston, John. *The Created Self: The Reader's Role in Eighteenth-Century Fiction*. London: Heineman, 1970.

Probyn, Clive T. *English Fiction of the Eighteenth Century, 1700–1789*. London and New York: Longman, 1987.

Richetti, John. *Popular Fiction before Richardson: Narrative Patterns, 1700–1739*. Oxford: Oxford University Press, 1969.

Spencer, Jane. *The Rise of the Woman Novelist: From Aphra Behn to Jane Austen*. Oxford and New York: Basil Blackwell, 1986.

Watt, Ian. *The Rise of the Novel: Studies in Defoe, Richardson, and Fielding*. Berkeley and Los Angeles: University of California Press, 1957.

INDIVIDUAL AUTHORS

DANIEL DEFOE

Bibliography

Stoler, John A. *Daniel Defoe: An Annotated Bibliography of Modern Criticism, 1900–1980*. New York and London: Garland Publishing, 1984.

Critical Studies

Backscheider, Paula R. *Daniel Defoe, His Life*. Baltimore and London: Johns Hopkins University Press, 1989.

Byrd, Max, ed. *Daniel Defoe: A Collection of Critical Essays*. Englewood Cliffs, N.J.: Prentice-Hall, 1976.

Hunter, J. Paul. *The Reluctant Pilgrim: Defoe's Emblematic Method and Quest for Form in "Robinson Crusoe."* Baltimore: Johns Hopkins University Press, 1966.

Novak, Maximillian. *Economics and the Fiction of Daniel Defoe*. Berkeley and Los Angeles: University of California Press, 1962.

Richetti, John. *Defoe's Narratives: Situations and Structures*. Oxford: Clarendon Press, 1975.

SAMUEL RICHARDSON

Bibliographies

Hannaford, Richard G. *Samuel Richardson: An Annotated Bibliography of Critical Studies.* New York and London: Garland Publishing, 1980. Covers 1740–1978.

Sale, William Merritt, Jr. *Samuel Richardson: A Bibliographical Record of His Literary Career with Historical Notes.* New Haven, Conn.: Yale University Press, 1936.

Critical Studies

Bloom, Harold, ed. *Modern Critical Views: Samuel Richardson.* New York: Chelsea House, 1987.

Castle, Terry. *Clarissa's Cyphers: Meaning and Disruption in Richardson's "Clarissa."* Ithaca, N.Y., and London: Cornell University Press, 1982.

Doody, Margaret. *A Natural Passion: A Study of the Novels of Samuel Richardson.* Oxford: Clarendon Press, 1974.

Duncan Eaves, T. C., and Ben D. Kimpel. *Samuel Richardson: A Biography.* Oxford: Clarendon Press, 1971.

Eagleton, Terry. *The Rape of Clarissa: Writing, Sexuality, and Class Struggle in Richardson.* Oxford and London: Basil Blackwell, 1982.

Kinkead-Weekes, Mark. *Samuel Richardson: Dramatic Novelist.* Ithaca, N.Y.: Cornell University Press, 1973.

Warner, William Beatty. *Reading "Clarissa": The Struggles of Interpretation.* New Haven and London: Yale University Press, 1979.

HENRY FIELDING

Bibliography

Stoler, John A., and Richard D. Fulton. *Henry Fielding: An Annotated Bibliography of Twentieth-Century Criticism, 1900–1977.* New York and London: Garland Publishing, 1980.

Critical Studies

Alter, Robert. *Fielding and the Nature of the Novel.* Cambridge, Mass.: Harvard University Press, 1968.

Battestin, Martin C. *Henry Fielding, A Life.* New York and London: Routledge, 1990.

―――. *The Moral Basis of Fielding's Art: A Study of "Joseph Andrews."* Middletown, Conn.: Wesleyan University Press, 1959. Not directly concerned with *Tom Jones* but does study the intellectual backgrounds of Fielding's thought.

Bloom, Harold, ed. *Modern Critical Interpretations: Henry Fielding's "Tom Jones."* New York: Chelsea House, 1987.

Hatfield, Glenn W. *Henry Fielding and the Language of Irony.* Chicago and London: University of Chicago Press, 1968.

Paulson, Ronald. *Satire and the Novel in Eighteenth-Century England.* New Haven, Conn.: Yale University Press, 1967.

LAURENCE STERNE

Bibliography

Hartley, Lodwick. *Sterne in the Twentieth Century: An Essay and a Bibliography of Sternean Studies, 1900–1965.* Chapel Hill: University of North Carolina Press, 1966.

Critical Studies

Alter, Robert. *Partial Magic: The Novel as a Self-conscious Genre.* Berkeley and Los Angeles: University of California Press, 1975. Includes a chapter on Sterne.
Byrd, Max. *"Tristram Shandy."* London: George Allen and Unwyn, 1985.
Cash, Arthur H. *Sterne: The Early and Middle Years.* London: Methuen, 1975. Another volume covering the rest of Sterne's life is promised.
Lanham, Richard. *"Tristram Shandy": The Games of Pleasure.* Berkeley and Los Angeles: University of California Press, 1973.
Traugott, John. *Tristram Shandy's World: Sterne's Philosophical Rhetoric.* Berkeley and Los Angeles: University of California Press, 1954.
————, ed. *Laurence Sterne: A Collection of Critical Essays.* Englewood Cliffs, N.J.: Prentice-Hall, 1968.

HORACE WALPOLE AND THE GOTHIC NOVEL

Bibliography

Sabor, Peter. *Horace Walpole: A Reference Guide.* Boston: G. K. Hall, 1984. Includes a bibliography of criticism through 1983.

Critical Studies

Kallich, Martin. *Horace Walpole.* New York: Twayne, 1971.
Kieley, Robert. *The Romantic Novel in England.* Cambridge, Mass.: Harvard University Press, 1972.
Lewis, W. S. *Horace Walpole.* New York: Pantheon, 1961.
Paulson, Ronald. *Representations of Revolution, 1789–1820.* New Haven, Conn.: Yale University Press, 1983.
Punter, David. *The Literature of Terror: A History of Gothic Fictions from 1765 to the Present Day.* London and New York: Longman, 1980.
Sedgwick, Eve Kosofsky. *The Coherence of Gothic Conventions.* New York: Arno Press, 1980.

JANE AUSTEN

Bibliographies

Gilson, David. *A Bibliography of Jane Austen.* Oxford: Clarendon Press, 1982. Complete through 1978.
Roth, Barry. *An Annotated Bibliography of Jane Austen Studies, 1973–83.* Charlottesville: University Press of Virginia, 1985.

Critical Studies

Butler, Marilyn. *Jane Austen and the War of Ideas*. Oxford: Oxford University Press, 1975.

Ehrenpreis, Irvin. *Acts of Implication: Suggestion and Covert Meaning in the Works of Dryden, Pope, Swift, and Austen*. Berkeley and Los Angeles: University of California Press, 1980.

Halperin, John. *The Life of Jane Austen*. Baltimore, Md.: Johns Hopkins University Press, 1984.

Hardy, Barbara. *A Reading of Jane Austen*. London: Peter Owen, 1975.

Tanner, Tony. *Jane Austen*. Cambridge, Mass.: Harvard University Press, 1986.

Thompson, James. *Between Self and World: The Novels of Jane Austen*. University Park, Pa., and London: Pennsylvania University Press, 1988.

Index